Developing
Professional Skills:
Environmental Law

Sandra B. Zellmer
University of Nebraska College of Law

Robert L. Glicksman
The George Washington University Law School

Series Editor: Colleen Medill

WEST
ACADEMIC
PUBLISHING

© 2016 LEG, Inc. d/b/a West Academic
    444 Cedar Street, Suite 700
    St. Paul, MN 55101
    1-877-888-1330

West, West Academic Publishing, and West Academic are trademarks of West Publishing Corporation, used under license.

Printed in the United States of America

ISBN: 978-0-314-28078-7

Acknowledgments

Model Rules of Professional Conduct ©2016 by the American Bar Association. Reprinted with permission. All rights reserved. This information or any portion thereof may not be copied or disseminated in any form or by any means or stored in an electronic database or retrieval system without the express consent of the American Bar Association.

Preface

LAW SCHOOLS ASPIRE to teach professional legal skills. Law schools today emphasize skills training more than ever before, in part in response to criticism that the traditional law school curriculum does not adequately prepare students for the practice of law. The soaring cost of law school tuition, coupled with the tight job market for law school graduates in recent years, has intensified the demand for skills training. Courses in pretrial advocacy, trial techniques, negotiation, and mediation are increasingly popular, as are clinical offerings.

Incorporating skills training into doctrinal law classes is challenging. Taking time for elaborate simulations can crowd out the coverage of fundamental legal concepts and doctrines, leaving both professors and students frustrated. Professors feel that there is never enough time to cover the subject matter adequately. Students feel there is never enough time, period.

Developing Professional Skills: Environmental Law is designed to provide skills training to students in a time-efficient manner. Each chapter in this book focuses on one or more of the following core legal skills:

- Client counseling (including engagement of a new client, interviewing, and correspondence);
- Factual development;
- Legal research;
- Legal drafting (including client correspondence via letters and emails, as well as traditional legal document drafting);
- Negotiation; and
- Advocacy

Although the length and complexity of the case studies in each chapter vary, students are expected to spend about three or four hours outside of the classroom preparing the skills assignment for each chapter. A comprehensive Teacher's Manual gives the professor guidance and discretion in determining how much classroom discussion time to devote to the material in each chapter. The professor may spend class time discussing the answer to the problem, and teasing out strengths and weakness of various approaches, strategies, and positions. This may entail role-playing and in-class exercises. In addition (or alternatively), the professor may focus on professional responsibility and the norms of modern legal practice. Selected provisions of the Model Rules of Professional Conduct, the Federal Rules of Civil Procedure, and the Administrative Procedure Act are provided in the Appendices of this book, along with client time sheets.

Developing Professional Skills: Environmental Law is intended to bring to life the materials taught in doctrinal environmental law classes, and several of the chapters are relevant for natural resources courses as well. The problems included in each chapter go well beyond the typical classroom experience of reading cases and answering questions. As lawyers, students will encounter idiosyncratic, demanding, and occasionally unreasonable or even unethical clients, novel legal problems, as well as ever-evolving technologies and old-fashioned financial and time management constraints. They will be required to engage in problem-solving, and to implement their solutions to these problems effectively and efficiently. While no book can truly simulate the nuanced tapestry that is modern legal practice, the exercises in this book can be used to enhance and enrich the students' educational experience and lead them one step closer to being practicing lawyers.

Several generous colleagues provided us with support and expertise in the writing of this book. As the creator of the *Developing Professional Skills* series, Colleen Medill, the Robert & Joanne Berkshire Family Professor of Law at the University of Nebraska, deserves a special shout-out for her encouragement and invitation to participate in this important and timely project. Brannon Denning and Michelle Harner, authors of *Developing Professional Skills: Environmental Law* and *Developing Professional Skills: Business Associations*, respectively, have our thanks for providing us with excellent models for upper-level offerings in this series. In addition, we are thankful to Seth Oranburg for his tips on email communications, and to Steve Schmidt and Randy Hill for sharing insights on our criminal law chapter.

We are also grateful to University of Nebraska College of Law for providing support through a summer research grant and sabbatical time, and The George Washington University Law School for support through a summer research grant. Last but far from least, our gratitude goes to Louis Higgins, Editor in Chief at West Academic Publishing, and Tessa Boury, Senior Acquisitions Editor, Foundation Press and West Academic Publishing, for nurturing this series and for giving us the opportunity to contribute to it.

Introduction

THE SKILLS NEEDED to practice environmental law are similar to the skills required for practicing law generally, so many of the exercises found in this book will be valuable for all sorts of law students. Environmental law, however, has some unique attributes, making the practice of environmental law unique and, compared to many other practice areas, diverse and cross-cutting.

First, environmental law is, for the most part, administrative law. Much of environmental law involves public law, rather than purely private law (although the common law tort underpinning of environmental law remains relevant, as Chapter 9 makes clear). As such, the powers and duties of governmental agencies and other public or quasi-public entities are often front and center in any environmental controversy. The rules of the road are prescribed, by and large, by the Administrative Procedure Act unless an agency's organic statute provides otherwise. Accordingly, this book is designed to develop the students' administrative practice skills.

Second, environmental cases typically involve the public interest. The standing of individuals and organizations is often based upon their claims as representatives of the public interest. Standing can be a significant impediment for many litigants, and various aspects of standing and other jurisdictional requirements encountered in the practice of environmental law are addressed in several chapters of this book.

Third, environmental cases often involve multiple parties. It is typical for a government agency, a regulated industry or developer, and an opponent to the issuance of a permit or the authorization of some activity that affects the environment all to be involved in administrative rulemaking, litigation in court, or other decisionmaking processes. Several of the exercises in this book involve multiple parties.

Fourth, environmental law is heavily inter-disciplinary. It is a rare environmental issue that does not implicate scientific issues, requiring lawyers to familiarize themselves with at least the basics of disciplines such as toxicology, hydrology, or epidemiology. Lawyers also must be able to determine when they need help from scientific experts in serving their clients' needs, and to identify and solicit the assistance of such experts. Several chapters in the book feature these challenges.

Finally, the resolution of environmental controversies, whether they involve the use of natural resources or the degradation of air, water, or soil, is often more permanent and wide-reaching than resolutions reached in private controversies involving economic or other interests of humans and human institutions. Rarely is monetary compensation adequate to redress an environmental harm. Several of the exercises included in this book touch upon the skills needed to seek or oppose injunctive relief.

Aside from the legal doctrinal and strategic considerations they present, these aspects of environmental practice may give rise to an array of ethical issues, such as conflicts of interest, client confidentiality, and deep-seated ideological differences. All of the chapters in this book invoke ethical issues and many raise potential ethical dilemmas. For ease of reference, the Appendix includes relevant provisions of the Model Rules of Professional Conduct, as well as the Federal Rules of Civil Procedure and the Administrative Procedure Act.

Students and professors alike should note that there are a variety of guidance documents and checklists relevant to the development of practice skills. A short compilation of checklists can be found online: *Checklist for the Client Letter or Memo*, The Writing Center, Georgetown University Law Center (2003), https://www.law.george-town.edu/academics/academic-programs/legal-writing-scholarship/writing-center/upload/checklistclient_000.pdf. Where relevant, other forms and checklists will be referenced throughout this book. When using checklists or forms, a "word to the wise" is in order. It is remarkably easy to follow a cookie-cutter approach when you've found an on-point form or list. Resist the temptation! Use caution. Be careful to think through your particular issue or case and to tailor the list or form accordingly.

Table of Contents

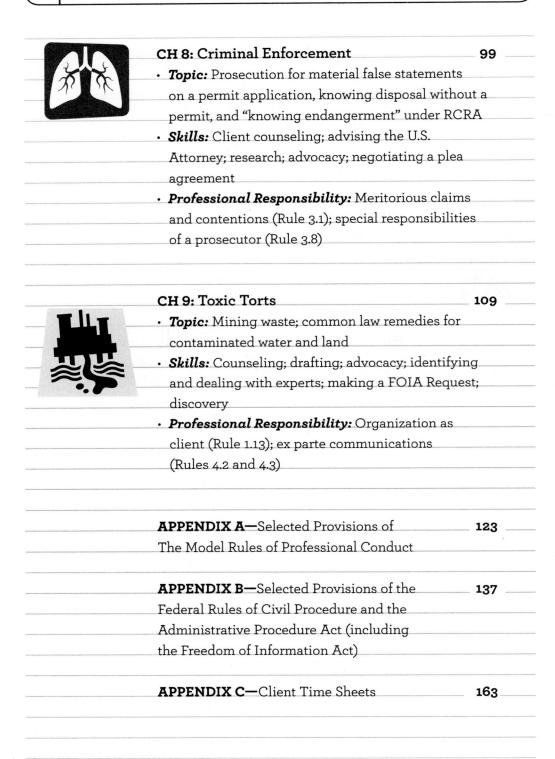

Developing Professional Skills:
ENVIRONMENTAL LAW

CHAPTER ONE

The Federal Register Is Your Friend
Commenting on Proposed Regulations

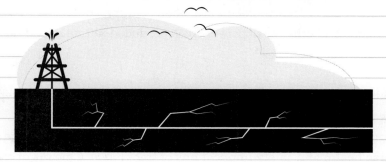

YOUR PRACTICE INVOLVES representation of a variety of small businesses. Among other things, you provide advice to them on the application of federal and state regulatory programs to their activities. Each day, one of the first things you do when you arrive at your office is to use your web browser to skim the table of contents of the Federal Register to see if that day's edition includes anything that may be of interest to any of your clients.

This morning, you noticed that the federal Environmental Protection Agency (EPA) has published an Advance Notice of Proposed Rulemaking, titled Hydraulic Fracturing Chemicals and Mixtures. In the Advance Notice, EPA explains that in response to a petition filed with it by several national public interest groups under § 21 of the Toxic Substances Control Act (TSCA), 15 U.S.C. § 2620, it has initiated a proceeding to consider whether to create a program for gathering information on the chemical substances and mixtures used in hydraulic fracturing. Hydraulic fracturing (sometimes known as fracking) is a technique for extracting natural gas in which fluids are injected through a wellbore into deep rock formations far beneath the surface. The fluids create pressure that cracks the rock in the forma-

tions, releasing natural gas that otherwise would have been trapped in the formation. The spread of fracking activity in recent years has greatly increased natural gas production in the United States, reducing natural gas prices and decreasing the country's dependence on natural gas and other energy resources produced in foreign, sometimes unstable countries.

Notwithstanding these benefits, considerable opposition has arisen to the use of fracking technologies. Local, regional, and national non-governmental organizations have expressed concern over the adverse health and safety implications of fracking as a means of extracting natural gas. As EPA explains in the Advance Notice, fracking opponents allege that the fluids that are injected into the wellbore contain potentially dangerous chemicals that can leak into adjacent groundwater aquifers, contaminating drinking water sources. In addition, the fracking fluids must be transported by truck to production sites, and the waste fluids extracted from the well after the fracking process must similarly be trucked away from production sites. Spills resulting from traffic accidents or during loading and unloading of the fracking fluids may create health risks to those owning or using neighboring properties.

EPA states in the Advance Notice that it is contemplating using its authority under § 8(a) and (d) of TSCA, 15 U.S.C. § 2607(a), (d), to adopt regulations that establish a process for generating and accumulating information on these health and safety risks so that the agency can determine whether it is appropriate to regulate the use of fracking fluids to alleviate these risks without sacrificing the energy-related benefits of fracking. Relevant portions of TSCA are provided at the end of this chapter.

EPA's regulatory authority under TSCA is derived from § 6(a), 15 U.S.C. § 2605(a), which authorizes EPA to regulate activities that pose an unreasonable risk of injury to health or the environment. TSCA does not define the term "unreasonable risk," but § 6(c)(1), 15 U.S.C. § 2605(c)(1), does specify considerations relevant to the adoption of regulations under § 6(a).

EPA's Advance Notice is of interest to you because you represent Chemicals Helping to Enhance Welfare (CHEW), a small, family-owned business that, among other things, manufactures fracking fluids. If EPA were to decide to regulate the manufacture, processing, distribution in commerce, use, or disposal of fracking fluids under § 6(a) of TSCA, CHEW would have to comply with those regulations. At a minimum, the regulations would likely increase CHEW's cost of doing business. They might even require dramatic changes in CHEW's operations if EPA decided to prohibit the manufacture or use of some types of fracking fluids that EPA regards as creating unreasonable risks of injury to health or the environment.

In its Advance Notice, EPA has solicited comments on a number of issues relating to its plan to consider the adoption of reporting requirements under TSCA § 8(d). You believe that it would behoove CHEW to submit comments in response to EPA's invitation. The Advance Notice states that

> EPA is requesting comment on the information that should be obtained or disclosed and the mechanism for obtaining or disclosing information about chemicals and mixtures used in hydraulic fracturing. This mechanism could be regulatory, voluntary, or a combination of both. EPA is also seeking comment on best management practices for the generation, collection, reporting and/or disclosure of public health and environmental information from or by companies that manufacture, process, or use chemical substances or mixtures in hydraulic fracturing activities—that is, practices or operations that can be implemented and verified toward achieving protection of public health and the environment—and whether voluntary certification, and

incentives for disclosure, could be valuable tools for improving chemical safety. In addition, the Agency is seeking comment on ways to minimize reporting burdens and costs, avoid duplication of efforts, and maximize transparency and public understanding. Finally, EPA is soliciting comments on incentives and recognition programs that could be used to support the development and use of safer chemicals in hydraulic fracturing.

In addition, EPA is seeking comment on a host of more specific questions. These are the ones that caught your eye:

- Should all information be required to be reported or should there be a voluntary mechanism for some or all information?

- What types of information, if any, should be required to be reported?

- How could incentives be structured to ensure effective voluntary disclosure of information on chemical substances and mixtures used in hydraulic fracturing?

- Should manufacturers (including importers), processors, or both be required to report under TSCA section 8(a)?

- Would manufacturers, service providers, well operators, or all three, know how a chemical substance or mixture is used at well sites? If all types of firms have this information, which type, if any, should be required to report?

- Are there thresholds that might be appropriate to limit reporting by small manufacturers or processors under either a regulatory or a voluntary program (e.g., the thresholds that define "small manufacturer" in 40 CFR §§ 704.3 and 712.25)? If so, how would the recommended reporting threshold affect cost to the reporting entity? How might different reporting thresholds affect the usefulness of the data provided?

- If a TSCA § 8(d) rule were promulgated, should it require reporting of studies for all chemical substances and mixtures used in hydraulic fracturing or only a subset? If only certain chemicals should be included in the rule, which ones should EPA include?

EPA has provided general guidance on the submission of comments, which are due in 90 days. The agency has explained:

> Comments should provide enough detail and contain sufficient supporting information in order for the Agency to understand the issues raised and give them the fullest consideration. Comments should include alternatives, rationales, benefits, technological and economic feasibility (including costs), and supporting data. Supporting information should include any information that substantiates your conclusions and recommendations, including, but not limited to: Experiences, data, analyses, studies and articles, and standard professional practices.

EPA, Advance Notice of Proposed Rulemaking, 79 Fed. Reg. 28664, 28666 (2014).

 ## Points to Consider

Task 1. You have decided that you should explain to CHEW's Chief Executive Officer, Casey Chew, how the process of submitting comments to EPA in response to an Advance Notice of Proposed Rulemaking works. Assume for purposes of this exercise that the procedures that apply to rulemaking conducted under TSCA are

those specified in § 553 of the federal Administrative Procedure Act (APA), 5 U.S.C. § 553, which is reproduced in part as Appendix B. Prepare a client letter describing to CEO Chew the process and the opportunities it provides to those interested in or affected by proposed agency regulations and why it would be a good idea for CHEW to take advantage of those opportunities. You might find the following checklist useful: *Checklist for the Client Letter or Memo*, The Writing Center, Georgetown University Law Center (2003), https://www.law. georgetown.edu/academics/academic-programs/legal-writing-scholar- ship/writing-center/upload/checklistclient_000.pdf.

Task 2. Assume that, after reading your letter, CEO Chew calls you and tells you he would like you to draft comments in response to EPA's Advance Notice of Proposed Rulemaking. He would like the com- ments to make the following points:

- There is insufficient evidence to support the conclusion that the use of fracking fluids poses any health, safety, or environmental risks. As a result, EPA should abandon its consideration of the creation of a reporting and information gathering program under TSCA § 8 for entities engaged in the manufacturing or processing of fracking fluids.

- If EPA decides to adopt a regulation under § 8 of TSCA, it should be entirely voluntary, not mandatory. Manufacturers of fracking fluids are good corporate citizens and have sufficient incentives to report in good faith without legal compulsion, including the desire to maintain good will among their customers and the public generally, and to provide safe workplaces for their employees.

- If EPA decides to adopt mandatory reporting requirements, it should exempt the specific chemicals manufactured by

CHEW because, even if other fracking fluids create health and environmental risks, the ones produced by CHEW do not.

- If EPA decides to adopt mandatory reporting requirements that cover the chemicals manufactured by CHEW, it should adopt threshold manufacturing volumes below which the reporting requirements would not apply. The rationale for such a threshold would be that companies that produce small amounts of fracking fluids pose de minimis health and safety risks that ought not to concern EPA, and the regulatory benefits of requiring reporting by manufacturers whose production levels are below the threshold would be outweighed by the burdens imposed on those manufacturers by a mandatory system. CHEW obviously wants the thresholds to be higher than the volume of fracking fluids it produces each year.

In the phone call, CEO Chew informed you that she did not believe that any of the chemicals used to produce CHEW's fracking fluids are in any way harmful to human health. In a subsequent phone conversation, however, CHEW's plant manager informed you that some of his workers have reported that, after handling some of the chemicals CHEW includes in its fracking fluids, they have experienced shortness of breath and skin rashes. According to the plant manager, he has received about ten such complaints since CHEW began producing fracking fluids five years ago. When you related this conversation to CEO Chew in a second phone call, Chew explained that she had not relayed this information to you earlier because she suspects that the employees who have made these complaints are trying to provide a basis for demanding wage increases to reflect the hazards they face on the job, and that the complaints are probably not legitimate. Chew indicated, however, that the company has not undertaken any studies, and she is not aware of any studies done by others, on whether the chemicals used to produce CHEW's fracking fluids pose health risks.

Task 3. Based on your analysis of the Advance Notice of Proposed Rulemaking, your conversations with CHEW's CEO and plant manager, and the relevant provisions of TSCA, which of the contentions that Chew wants to make should you include in the comments you draft? Be sure to consider the provisions of the Model Code of Professional Responsibility that appear in Appendix A. In particular, take note of:

- Rule 1.2 Scope of Representation and Allocation of Authority Between Client and Lawyer
- Rule 1.4 Communication
- Rule 2.1 Advisor
- Rule 3.1 Meritorious Claims and Contentions
- Rule 3.3 Candor Toward the Tribunal
- Rule 4.1 Truthfulness in Statements to Others

Task 4. Based on your analysis of the matters referred to in point 2 above, prepare draft comments to be submitted to EPA on the issues you have decided to address on behalf of CHEW. To the extent the comments will require information you do not currently have, include bracketed descriptions to CEO Chew of the information you need the company to provide to you to bolster the points you intend to make and describe why that information is relevant and important if the comments are going to successfully advance the client's interests. Be sure to refer to the deadline for submitting comments in response to the Advance Notice of Proposed Rulemaking and propose a schedule for CHEW to return an edited draft to you so that you will have time to review CHEW's edit and solicit additional information, if necessary, before finalizing and submitting the comments.

Task 5. When you have completed drafting CHEW's comments, go to EPA's website and determine the best way to submit the comments to the agency.

> The Toxic Substances Control Act

TSCA § 3, 15 U.S.C. § 2602. Definitions

. . .

(6) The term "health and safety study" means any study of any effect of a chemical substance or mixture on health or the environment or on both, including underlying data and epidemiological studies, studies of occupational exposure to a chemical substance or mixture, toxicological, clinical, and ecological studies of a chemical substance or mixture, and any test performed pursuant to this chapter.

TSCA § 6, 15 U.S.C. § 2605.
Regulation of Hazardous Chemical Substances and Mixtures

(a) Scope of regulation

If the Administrator finds that there is a reasonable basis to conclude that the manufacture, processing, distribution in commerce, use, or disposal of a chemical substance or mixture, or that any combination of such activities, presents or will present an unreasonable risk of injury to health or the environment, the Administrator shall by rule apply one or more of the following requirements to such substance or mixture to the extent necessary to protect adequately against such risk using the least burdensome requirements:

    (1) A requirement (A) prohibiting the manufacturing, processing, or distribution in commerce of such substance or mixture, or (B) limiting the amount of such substance or mixture which may be manufactured, processed, or distributed in commerce.

    (2) A requirement—

        (A) prohibiting the manufacture, processing, or distribution in commerce of such substance or mixture for (i) a particular use or (ii) a particular use in a concentration in excess of a level specified by the Administrator in the rule imposing the requirement, or

(B) limiting the amount of such substance or mixture which may be manufactured, processed, or distributed in commerce for (i) a particular use or (ii) a particular use in a concentration in excess of a level specified by the Administrator in the rule imposing the requirement.

(3) A requirement that such substance or mixture or any article containing such substance or mixture be marked with or accompanied by clear and adequate warnings and instructions with respect to its use, distribution in commerce, or disposal or with respect to any combination of such activities. The form and content of such warnings and instructions shall be prescribed by the Administrator.

(4) A requirement that manufacturers and processors of such substance or mixture make and retain records of the processes used to manufacture or process such substance or mixture and monitor or conduct tests which are reasonable and necessary to assure compliance with the requirements of any rule applicable under this subsection.

(5) A requirement prohibiting or otherwise regulating any manner or method of commercial use of such substance or mixture.

(6) (A) A requirement prohibiting or otherwise regulating any manner or method of disposal of such substance or mixture, or of any article containing such substance or mixture, by its manufacturer or processor or by any other person who uses, or disposes of, it for commercial purposes.

(B) A requirement under subparagraph (A) may not require any person to take any action which would be in violation of any law or requirement of, or in effect for, a State or political subdivision, and shall require each person subject to it to notify each State and political subdivision in which a required disposal may occur of such disposal.

(7) A requirement directing manufacturers or processors of such substance or mixture (A) to give notice of such unreasonable risk of injury to distributors in commerce of such substance or mixture and, to the extent reasonably ascertainable, to other persons in possession of such substance or mixture or exposed to such substance or mixture, (B) to give public notice of such risk of injury, and (C) to replace or repurchase such substance or mixture as elected by the person to which the requirement is directed.

Any requirement (or combination of requirements) imposed under this subsection may be limited in application to specified geographic areas. . . .

(c) Promulgation of subsection (a) rules

(1) In promulgating any rule under subsection (a) of this section with respect to a chemical substance or mixture, the Administrator shall consider and publish a statement with respect to—

(A) the effects of such substance or mixture on health and the magnitude of the exposure of human beings to such substance or mixture,

(B) the effects of such substance or mixture on the environment and the magnitude of the exposure of the environment to such substance or mixture,

(C) the benefits of such substance or mixture for various uses and the availability of substitutes for such uses, and

(D) the reasonably ascertainable economic consequences of the rule, after consideration of the effect on the national economy, small business, technological innovation, the environment, and public health. . . .

TSCA § 8, 15 U.S.C. § 2607.
Reporting and Retention of Information

(a) Reports

(1) The Administrator shall promulgate rules under which—

(A) each person (other than a small manufacturer or processor) who manufactures or processes or proposes to manufacture or process a chemical substance (other than a chemical substance described in subparagraph (B)(ii)) shall maintain such records, and shall submit to the Administrator such reports, as the Administrator may reasonably require, and

(B) each person (other than a small manufacturer or processor) who manufactures or processes or proposes to manufacture or process—

(i) a mixture, or

(ii) a chemical substance in small quantities (as defined by the Administrator by rule) solely for purposes of scientific experimentation or analysis or chemical research on, or analysis of, such substance or another substance, including any such research or analysis for the development of a product,

shall maintain records and submit to the Administrator reports but only to the extent the Administrator determines the maintenance of records or submission of reports, or both, is necessary for the effective enforcement of this chapter. . . .

(2) The Administrator may require under paragraph (1) maintenance of records and reporting with respect to the following insofar as known to the person making the report or insofar as reasonably ascertainable:

(A) The common or trade name, the chemical identity, and the molecular structure of each chemical substance or mixture for which such a report is required.

(B) The categories or proposed categories of use of each such substance or mixture.

(C) The total amount of each such substance and mixture manufactured or processed, reasonable estimates of the total amount to be manufactured or processed, the amount manufactured or processed for each of its categories of use, and reasonable estimates of the amount to be manufactured or processed for each of its categories of use or proposed categories of use.

(D) A description of the byproducts resulting from the manufacture, processing, use, or disposal of each such substance or mixture.

(E) All existing data concerning the environmental and health effects of such substance or mixture.

(F) The number of individuals exposed, and reasonable estimates of the number who will be exposed, to such substance or mixture in their places of employment and the duration of such exposure. . . .

(G) In the initial report under paragraph (1) on such substance or mixture, the manner or method of its disposal, and in any subsequent report on such substance or mixture, any change in such manner or method. . . .

(d) Health and safety studies

The Administrator [of EPA] shall promulgate rules under which the Administrator shall require any person who manufactures, processes, or distributes in commerce or who proposes to manufacture, process, or distribute in commerce any chemical substance or mixture (or with respect to paragraph (2), any person who has possession of a study) to submit to the Administrator—

(1) lists of health and safety studies (A) conducted or initiated by or for such person with respect to such substance or mixture at any time, (B) known to such person, or (C) reasonably ascertainable by such person, except that the Administrator may exclude certain types or categories of studies from the requirements of this subsection if the Administrator finds that submission of lists of such studies are unnecessary to carry out the purposes of this chapter; and

(2) copies of any study contained on a list submitted pursuant to paragraph (1) or otherwise known by such person. . . .

CHAPTER TWO

The Endangered Species Act

Jumping Through Hoops and
Being a Competent Representative

A FRIEND OF A FRIEND OF YOURS, Olivia Green, recently contacted you and invited you to join her for lunch. Olivia has just been elected as the new director of the nonprofit group Oregon Coast Advocates (OCA), which engages in outreach, advocacy, and educational activities along the Oregon coast. She heard that you're an outdoor enthusiast and, best of all, that you occasionally accept pro bono clients. While munching on her vegan sandwich, Olivia describes a situation that's extremely worrisome to herself and other members of OCA.

Darth V. Corporation plans to engage in mineral development on land that it purchased on the Oregon coast last year. Darth believes that lucrative deposits of molybdenum are located in and around its property. Molybdenum, a silvery metal, is a rare earth material used in high-strength steel alloys for industrial and military applications. About two-thirds of all the molybdenum in the world comes from Canada, China, and the United States.

Darth's plan calls for surveys and extensive earth-moving to find and develop the minerals. A dozen or so crew members, working with off-road vehicles, will remove vegetation, dig into the earth, and place geological equipment in strategic locations to determine the presence of molybdenum. When deposits are found, full scale extraction operations will commence, involving a great deal of disturbance to soil and vegetation. If all goes well for Darth, the property will be completely leveled and denuded by the conclusion of operations, and Darth hopes to sell it to a residential developer.

Darth's property provides suitable habitat for four federally endangered or threatened species: Canada lynx; Oregon spotted frog; western snowy (coastal) plover; and short-tailed albatross. Because Darth needed a Clean Water Act Section 404 permit from the U.S. Army Corps of Engineers to disturb wetlands on the property in conjunction with the mining plan, the Corps consulted with the U.S. Fish & Wildlife Service (FWS) about the potential impacts on species, and the FWS issued a biological opinion (BO).

According to the BO, neither the lynx nor the frog had been spotted on the parcel since Darth purchased it, so the BO found "no jeopardy" as to those two species. However, both bird species have been seen foraging, roosting, and nesting on the parcel. The BO imposed seasonal restrictions on Darth's operating plan to minimize effects on bird species during the nesting season. Darth will avoid nesting areas during May, which is the most critical time for the birds, although nesting sometimes occurs in April and June as well. Accordingly, the FWS issued a "no jeopardy" opinion as to these species and gave Darth an incidental take permit (ITP) in case any plovers or albatross were harmed.

On behalf of OCA, Olivia seeks your legal services. She explains that OCA can't pay you anything up front, but if you win, you may be entitled to recover your legal fees and costs under the ESA's citizen suit provision. OCA would like to prevent Darth from going forward with its plan because it fears that Darth's activities will cause visual impacts, noise, pollution, and disruption of wildlife. Now that the BO has been issued, Darth intends to move forward with exploration plans immediately.

 ## Points to Consider

At present, OCA isn't interested in asserting any Clean Water Act claims; rather, it wants to bring an ESA suit against both Darth and the FWS. You've never handled an ESA issue before, and you never even took a class on the subject, but you believe you can get up to speed without investing much time and effort. After lunch, you take an hour or so to peruse the statute, and you find the relevant statutory provisions (provided below).

In addition to familiarizing yourself with the relevant statutory provisions, your representation of OCA will trigger several tasks.

Task 1. Should you take this case? Are there any potential ethical quandaries involved? Consider Model Rules 1.1, 1.3, and 6.1, provided in Appendix A.

Task 2. Make a list of the documents you believe you'll need from Darth and/or FWS, and note how you'll obtain them. Is everything likely to be included in the agency's administrative record? Can you think of any relevant information you might wish to obtain from other persons or entities?

Task 3. Write an email to your client, advising OCA about the possibility of stopping Darth before any disturbance occurs, and about any relevant legal impediments OCA may face if it ultimately proceeds with a lawsuit seeking injunctive relief. Take a look at 16 U.S.C. 1540(g) provided below, and FRCP 65, provided in Appendix B.

A cautionary note regarding emails: Communicating via email is quicker and cheaper than a formal legal memorandum. The idea is to convey a lot of information clearly with a minimum of words. It's important to remember that people read on-screen materials, like emails, differently than letters and memos. It's natural to skim emails rather than giving them the time and attention that other types of communications might warrant, and readers tend to be more susceptible to distractions while reading emails. From your standpoint, as the writer, be aware of—and resist—the psychological "online dis-inhibition effect," which leads people to abandon social inhibitions online. As lawyers, we have to pay careful attention to what we write, whether it's an email or some other form of communication. In a way, you should be even more careful with emails than with letters to your client, because it's all too easy for the recipient to hit "forward," sending your email off to all sorts of unintended places in a nanosecond.

As you draft your email, consult the following checklist. For a more detailed checklist on emailing clients, see RICHARD NEUMANN AND KRISTEN KONRAD TISCIONE, LEGAL REASONING AND LEGAL WRITING, 234-236 (7th ed. 2013).

Email Checklist*

❑ Identify your topic on the "re" line. The subject should be briefly descriptive yet non-confidential.

❑ Start with a simple salutation, such as "Dear Client" or "Good morning, Client."

❑ Use a brief closing, *e.g.,* "Sincere regards," and your name.

❑ Use a relatively informal yet professional tone.

❑ Avoid happy faces and other emoticons; they're not cool in this context.

❑ Make the email long enough to convey the subject, but be succinct and get to the point without embellishment. Anything over two pages or 8,000 characters is too long. (If you're conveying in-depth legal advice, an email may not be the best way to do it.)

❑ Ask the necessary questions and clearly articulate your "bottom-line" answer. Clients are busy people; avoid leaving things for unnecessary follow-up emails.

❑ Be sure to attach any "attachments" (they're easy to forget).

❑ Proofread for errors before hitting "send."

* SETH ORANBURG, LEGAL WRITING 1–3 (2015).

Task 4. Draft an appropriate notice letter on behalf of OCA. A template is provided below.

Sample ESA 60-Day Notice Letter

[YOUR LETTERHEAD & ADDRESS]
[DATE]
[VIA CERTIFIED MAIL, RETURN RECEIPT REQUESTED]

RECIPIENTS:

[Secretary of the Dept. of Interior]
[Assistant Secretary of the Dept. of Interior U.S. Fish and Wildlife Service]
[Private Party/Permittee]

RE: *Notice of Intent to Sue for Violations of the Endangered Species Act Regarding* [SPECIES OF CONCERN]

Dear [Recipients]:

In accordance with the 60-day notice requirement of the Endangered Species Act (ESA), 16 U.S.C. 1540(g), I hereby provide notice of intent to sue for violations of section[s] X X X of the ESA relating to X X X.

[FACTUAL BACKGROUND—*In as much detail as possible, describe the facts supporting the allegations of violations of the ESA's requirements or prohibitions: who; what; when; where; how.*]

60-Day Notice Letter, continued

[VIOLATIONS OF THE ESA—*Connect the dots by spelling out each statutory section you believe has been violated, and synthesize those provisions with the pertinent facts described above. Be succinct, but be thorough.*]

[PARTY GIVING NOTICE—*Yes, your contact information is provided in your letterhead, but provide details here.*]

[RELIEF DEMANDED—*What do you expect to demand in your complaint, if it comes to that? What do you want the agency or other alleged violator to do to comply with the law?*]

If you wish to discuss this matter further, please contact me at the address provided above.

Sincerely,

[NAME AND CONTACT INFORMATION]

> The Endangered Species Act (ESA)

ESA § 7, 16 U.S.C. § 1536. Prohibited Acts

* * *

(a)(2) Each Federal agency shall, in consultation with and with the assistance of the Secretary, insure that any action authorized, funded, or carried out by such agency . . . is not likely to jeopardize the continued existence of any endangered species or threatened species. . . . In fulfilling the requirements of this paragraph each agency shall use the best scientific and commercial data available. . . .

(b)(3)(A) Promptly after conclusion of consultation [under paragraph (a)(2)] . . . , the Secretary shall provide to the Federal agency and the applicant, if any, a written statement setting forth the Secretary's opinion, and a summary of the information on which the opinion is based, detailing how the agency action affects the species. . . . If jeopardy or adverse modification is found, the Secretary shall suggest those reasonable and prudent alternatives which he believes would not violate subsection (a)(2) of this section and can be taken by the Federal agency or applicant in implementing the agency action. . . .

(b)(4) If after consultation under subsection (a)(2) of this section, the Secretary concludes that—

(A) the agency action will not violate such subsection, or offers reasonable and prudent alternatives which the Secretary believes would not violate such subsection; [and]

(B) the taking of an endangered species or a threatened species incidental to the agency action will not violate such subsection. . . .

the Secretary shall provide the Federal agency and the applicant concerned, if any, with a written statement that—

(i) specifies the impact of such incidental taking on the species,

(ii) specifies those reasonable and prudent measures that the Secretary considers necessary or appropriate to minimize such impact, . . . and

(iv) sets forth the terms and conditions . . . that must be complied with by the Federal agency or applicant (if any), or both, to implement the measures specified under clause[] (ii). . . .

ESA § 9, 16 U.S.C. § 1538. Prohibited Acts

(a)(1)(B) Except as [otherwise] provided . . . , with respect to any endangered species of fish or wildlife listed pursuant to section 1533 of this title it is unlawful for any person subject to the jurisdiction of the United States to . . . take any such species. . . .

ESA § 10, 16 U.S.C. § 1539. Exceptions

(a)(1) The Secretary may permit, under such terms and conditions as he shall prescribe . . .

(B) any taking otherwise prohibited by section 1538(a) (1) (B) of this title if such taking is incidental to, and not the purpose of, the carrying out of an otherwise lawful activity.

(2) (A) No permit may be issued by the Secretary authorizing any taking referred to in paragraph (1) (B) unless the applicant therefor submits to the Secretary a conservation plan that specifies—

(i) the impact which will likely result from such taking;

(ii) what steps the applicant will take to minimize and mitigate such impacts, and the funding that will be available to implement such steps;

(iii) what alternative actions to such taking the applicant considered and the reasons why such alternatives are not being utilized; and

(iv) such other measures that the Secretary may require as being necessary or appropriate for purposes of the plan.

(B) If the Secretary finds, after opportunity for public comment, with respect to a permit application and the related conservation plan that—

(i) the taking will be incidental;

(ii) the applicant will, to the maximum extent practicable, minimize and mitigate the impacts of such taking;

(iii) the applicant will ensure that adequate funding for the plan will be provided;

(iv) the taking will not appreciably reduce the likelihood of the survival and recovery of the species in the wild; and

v) the measures, if any, required under subparagraph (A) (iv) will be met . . . , the Secretary shall issue the permit. The permit shall contain such terms and conditions as the Secretary deems necessary or appropriate to carry out the purposes of this paragraph. . . .

ESA § 11, 16 U.S.C. § 1540(g). Citizen Suits

(1) Except as provided in paragraph (2) of this subsection any person may commence a civil suit on his own behalf—

(A) to enjoin any person, including the United States and any other governmental instrumentality or agency (to the extent permitted by the eleventh amendment to the Constitution), who is alleged to be in violation of any provision of this chapter or regulation issued under the authority thereof; or

(B) to compel the Secretary to apply . . . The prohibitions set forth in or authorized pursuant to section . . . 1538(a) (1) (B) of this title with respect to the taking of any resident endangered species or threatened species within any State. . . . In any civil suit commenced under subparagraph (B) the district court shall compel the Secretary to apply the prohibition sought if the court finds that the allegation that an emergency exists is supported by substantial evidence. . . .

(2) (A) No action may be commenced under subparagraph (1)(A) of this section—

(i) prior to sixty days after written notice of the violation has been given to the Secretary, and to any alleged violator of any such provision or regulation. . . .

(B) No action may be commenced under subparagraph (1)(B) of this section—

(i) prior to sixty days after written notice has been given to the Secretary setting forth the reasons why an emergency is thought to exist with respect to an endangered species or a threatened species in the State concerned. . . .

(4) The court, in issuing any final order in any suit brought pursuant to paragraph (1) of this subsection, may award costs of litigation (including reasonable attorney and expert witness fees) to any party, whenever the court determines such award is appropriate.

(5) The injunctive relief provided by this subsection shall not restrict any right which any person (or class of persons) may have under any statute or common law to seek enforcement of any standard or limitation or to seek any other relief (including relief against the Secretary or a State agency).

CHAPTER THREE

The National Environmental Policy Act (NEPA)

Motion to Dismiss for Lack of Jurisdiction

YOUR CLIENT, TransGas Transmission Co. (TTC), has received a conditional certificate of public convenience and necessity from the Federal Energy Regulatory Commission (FERC). The certificate authorizes TTC to extend a natural gas pipeline across southern Ohio. TTC's proposal would involve the construction of approximately 19 miles of 26-inch diameter pipeline between a newly constructed TTC terminus and an existing TTC compressor station. This $120 million project is part of a system-wide $2 billion, three-year modernization program designed to improve TTC's aging infrastructure in the region. TTC claims that its customers are susceptible to outages if service is required to be interrupted for repairs or maintenance because TTC has only a single pipeline in this corridor, and because no other pipelines in the area have the necessary capacity to provide replacement gas deliveries. Although neither the public nor FERC is aware of this at the moment, your client has informed you in confidence that it intends to build another new high capacity pipeline in southern Ohio to transport oil or gas from a nearby well field it is beginning to develop through hydro-fracturing. If all goes as planned, TTC would seek approval for that pipeline within the next 12 months.

As background, the certificate is required by the Natural Gas Act (NGA), which requires any party seeking to construct a facility for transporting natural gas to obtain such a certificate before moving forward with the project. FERC may grant a certificate only if the project "is or will be required by the present or future public convenience and necessity." 15 U.S.C. § 717f. More specifically, in deciding whether to authorize the construction of major natural gas pipelines, FERC must balance public benefits against potential adverse consequences, giving appropriate consideration to the enhancement of competitive alternatives, whether the company can financially support the project, the possibility of overbuilding, the avoidance of unnecessary disruptions of the environment, and the unneeded exercise of eminent domain.

Although the project will disturb 310 acres of land, to minimize impacts on landowners, TTC will construct the pipeline primarily on existing rights-of-way and areas adjacent to existing rights-of-way. In issuing its certificate, FERC found that TTC had designed the project to minimize adverse impacts on landowners and surrounding communities, that TTC was fiscally responsible, that the project is necessary not to add capacity to TTC's system but to increase system reliability and operational flexibility, and that the pipeline satisfied all other relevant requirements of the Natural Gas Act.

In issuing a certificate, FERC must also comply with a variety of other federal laws, including the separate statutory mandate of the National Environmental Policy Act (NEPA), which requires an environmental analysis for "major Federal actions." 42 U.S.C. § 4332(2)(C). Instead of preparing a lengthy and time-consuming Environmental Impact Statement (EIS), FERC prepared a 25-page Environmental Assessment (EA) and a Finding of No Significant Impact (FONSI) for the pipeline project. The EA covered impacts to soils, water resources, wetlands, vegetation, fisheries, wildlife, land use, visual resources, air quality, noise, safety, and cumulative impacts, and dismissed them as inconsequential. It also assessed the Action Alternative (TTC's application for a FERC certificate to construct the pipeline) and one other alternative (No Action, i.e., no new pipeline construction). The EA concluded that the project's construction and operation would not significantly impact the quality of the environment, and that no additional alternatives needed to be considered. FERC also considered the comments received during the public scoping review, including comments lodged by a local landowners' group called Not in My Backyard (NIMBY), but dismissed the issues raised by the public as duplicative of issues raised by FERC itself and thoroughly addressed in the EA in the course of assessing the certificate's impacts. NIMBY made only one observation that was unique to its comments: that an alternative route should have been considered that avoided use of their properties. NIMBY failed to say where, exactly, such a route might be located.

The issuance of the conditional certificate (based on the analysis of the EA) enables TTC to exercise the power of eminent domain to obtain the necessary rights-of-way to construct, operate, and maintain the pipeline. 15 U.S.C. § 171f(h). NIMBY has filed suit in federal district court to challenge the issuance of the certificate, claiming its members are suffering or will imminently suffer harm because their property  lies along the proposed pipeline route and thus is subject to eminent domain proceedings by TTC. Along with its complaint against FERC, NIMBY has petitioned for a preliminary injunction against the exercise of eminent domain, and has submitted affidavits of members alleging concerns about contamination of their property from pipeline construction and operation, impacts on wetlands, fish, wildlife, and vegetation, forest fragmentation, and impacts on several species of game birds that NIMBY's members like to hunt during the game season.

NIMBY's arguments are centered on NEPA rather than the NGA. NIMBY alleges that FERC violated NEPA in issuing the certificate by issuing an EA rather than a full-blown EIS. In NIMBY's view, FERC's finding that the proposal would have no significant environmental impacts was arbitrary and capricious. In addition, NIMBY argues that FERC improperly "segmented" TTC's pipeline proposal by ignoring the pipeline's connection to the system-wide modernization project's impacts; in doing so, FERC obfuscated the cumulative impacts of the overall project.

NEPA itself says very little about the process or substance of the requisite environmental analysis. The Council for Environmental Quality (CEQ), which is responsible for supervising compliance with NEPA by other federal agencies, has issued detailed regulations to aid in the implementation of NEPA, so you'll need to turn your attention to the Code of Federal Regulations (C.F.R.), in which those regulations appear. The relevant statutory and regulatory provisions are provided below.

 Points to Consider

NIMBY's lawsuit threatens TTC's interest in moving forward with the pipeline in a timely fashion and in keeping its system-wide modernization project on track. In addition to familiarizing yourself with the relevant regulatory provisions of NEPA and the CEQ regulations, your representation of TTC triggers several tasks.

Task 1. Advise TTC regarding the likelihood of being granted intervention in NIMBY's lawsuit. Of course, TTC believes that the EA that FERC prepared is perfectly adequate, so advise your client whether intervention in this proceeding is an appropriate use of its resources when FERC is likely to defend the EA vigorously. Be prepared to satisfy the requirements of Fed. R. Civ. P. 24:

> ▶ **Rule 24. Intervention**
>
> 1. *Intervention of Right.* On timely motion, the court must permit anyone to intervene who . . . claims an interest relating to the property or transaction that is the subject of the action, and is so situated that disposing of the action may as a practical matter impair or impede the movant's ability to protect its interest, unless existing parties adequately represent that interest.
>
> 2. *Permissive Intervention.* On timely motion, the court may permit anyone to intervene who . . . has a claim or defense that shares with the main action a common question of law or fact. . . . In exercising its discretion, the court must consider whether the intervention will unduly delay or prejudice the adjudication of the original parties' rights.
>
> 3. *Notice and Pleading Required.* . . . The motion must state the grounds for intervention and be accompanied by a pleading that sets out the claim or defense for which intervention is sought.

Task 2. TTC is interested in disposing of this lawsuit as quickly and efficiently as possible. Are there any jurisdictional grounds on which TTC might seek dismissal? In particular, does NIMBY have constitutional standing (in short, a concrete injury in fact with a causal connection to the EA and that is redressable by a court)? See Lujan v. Defenders of Wildlife, 504 U.S. 555, 560 (1992); Hunt v. Wash. State Apple Comm'n, 432 U.S. 333, 342–43 (1977). If not, draft a motion to dismiss based on lack of standing. A sample is provided at the end of this chapter.

Task 3. Does NIMBY have prudential standing, in other words, is it within the zone of interests of NEPA? Note that, unlike the Endangered Species Act, the Clean Water Act, and many other environmental statutes, NEPA does not contain a citizen suit provision. As a result, parties involved in NEPA litigation must sue under the Administrative Procedure Act's general provisions for challenging final agency action. *See* 5 U.S.C. §§ 702, 704 and 706 (in Appendix B of this book). Section 702 limits judicial review to persons who are "adversely affected or aggrieved by agency action within the meaning of a relevant statute." Are NIMBY's claims more likely to frustrate than effectuate NEPA's purposes? Are the asserted injuries purely economic? If so, is NIMBY an appropriate representative of the environmental interests underlying the statute? *See* Bennett v. Spear, 520 U.S. 154 (1997); Nat'l Ass'n of Home Builders v. U.S. Army Corps of Engineers, 417 F.3d 1272, 1287 (D.C. Cir. 2005). If not, revise your motion to dismiss and add lack of prudential standing as a ground for dismissal of NIMBY's lawsuit.

Task 4. Do NIMBY's NEPA claims seek to challenge "final agency action"? 5 U.S.C. § 704; Norton v. S. Utah Wilderness Alliance, 542 U.S. 55 (2004). Are they ripe for judicial review? Ripeness requires courts to consider "the fitness of the issues for judicial review and the hardship to the parties of withholding court consideration." Abbot Laboratories v. Gardner, 387 U.S. 136 (1967); Lujan v. Nat'l Wildlife Fed'n, 497 U.S. 871 (1990); Nat'l Ass'n of Home Builders v. U.S. Army Corps of

Engineers, 417 F.3d 1272, 1281-1282 (D.C. Cir. 2005). If the claims are deficient in these aspects, revise your motion to dismiss accordingly.

Task 5. In a memo to the client, provide TTC with an assessment of the merits of NIMBY's NEPA claims in the event that jurisdictional hurdles are overcome. In particular, consider the adequacy of the EA and FONSI, given the scale of the project and its potential connection to other related actions, and the adequacy of the alternatives discussed in the EA. Be sure to apply the relevant factors of 40 C.F.R. 1508.27. With respect to the possibility of another new pipeline in the near future, you should also consider Rules 1.6, 2.1, and 3.3 of the Model Rules of Professional Responsibility (provided in Appendix A of this book).

> NEPA

42 U.S.C. § 4332(2)(C)

[A]ll agencies of the Federal Government shall . . . include in every recommendation or report on proposals for legislation and other major Federal actions significantly affecting the quality of the human environment, a detailed statement by the responsible official on—

(i) the environmental impact of the proposed action,

(ii) any adverse environmental effects which cannot be avoided should the proposal be implemented,

(iii) alternatives to the proposed action,

(iv) the relationship between local short-term uses of man's environment and the maintenance and enhancement of long-term productivity, and

(v) any irreversible and irretrievable commitments of resources which would be involved in the proposed action should it be implemented.

> NEPA Regulations

40 C.F.R. § 1502.14.
Alternatives including the proposed action.

[The agency] . . . should present the environmental impacts of the proposal and the alternatives in comparative form, thus sharply defining the issues and providing a clear basis for choice among options by the decisionmaker and the public. In this section agencies shall:

(a) Rigorously explore and objectively evaluate all reasonable alternatives. . .

(b) Devote substantial treatment to each alternative considered in detail including the proposed action so that reviewers may evaluate their comparative merits. . . [and]

(d) Include the alternative of no action. . . .

40 C.F.R. § 1508.9. Environmental Assessment.

Environmental Assessment:

(a) Means a concise public document for which a Federal agency is responsible that serves to . . .

(1) Briefly provide sufficient evidence and analysis for determining whether to prepare an environmental impact statement or a finding of no significant impact. . . .

40 C.F.R. § 1508.27. Significantly.

"Significantly" as used in NEPA requires considerations of both context and intensity:

(a) *Context.* This means that the significance of an action must be analyzed in several contexts such as society as a whole (human, national), the affected region, the affected interests, and the locality. Significance varies with the setting of the proposed action. For instance, in the case of a site-specific action, significance would usually depend upon the effects in the locale rather than in the world as a whole. Both short- and long-term effects are relevant.

(b) *Intensity.* This refers to the severity of impact. . . . The following should be considered in evaluating intensity:

(1) Impacts that may be both beneficial and adverse. A significant effect may exist even if the Federal agency believes that on balance the effect will be beneficial.

(2) The degree to which the proposed action affects public health or safety.

(3) Unique characteristics of the geographic area such as proximity to historic or cultural resources, park lands, prime farmlands, wetlands, wild and scenic rivers, or ecologically critical areas.

(4) The degree to which the effects on the quality of the human environment are likely to be highly controversial.

(5) The degree to which the possible effects on the human environment are highly uncertain or involve unique or unknown risks.

(6) The degree to which the action may establish a precedent for future actions with significant effects or represents a decision in principle about a future consideration.

(7) Whether the action is related to other actions with individually insignificant but cumulatively significant impacts. Significance exists if it is reasonable to anticipate a cumulatively significant impact on the environment. Significance cannot be avoided by terming an action temporary or by breaking it down into small component parts.

(8) The degree to which the action may adversely affect districts, sites, highways, structures, or objects listed in or eligible for listing in the National Register of Historic Places or may cause loss or destruction of significant scientific, cultural, or historical resources.

(9) The degree to which the action may adversely affect an endangered or threatened species or its habitat that has been determined to be critical under the Endangered Species Act of 1973.

(10) Whether the action threatens a violation of Federal, State, or local law or requirements imposed for the protection of the environment.

* * *

Sample Motion to Dismiss

IN THE (*Name of Court Here*)

_____

(*Name of Plaintiff Here*),	)	
Plaintiff,	)	
	)	CIVIL
vs.	)	
	)	
(*Your Client's Name(s) Here*),	)	Case No.: ____
	)	
Defendant(s).	)	

_____

MOTION TO DISMISS PLAINTIFF'S COMPLAINT

Defendant(s) (Name(s) Here), file this Motion to Dismiss Plaintiff's complaint and as grounds therefore state(s):

1. Plaintiff has filed a lawsuit seeking (*identify the cause of action*).

2. Plaintiff's complaint should be dismissed for failure to state a cause of action and for lack of subject matter jurisdiction.

3. (*Describe grounds for dismissal for failure to state a claim under 12(b)(6). This will likely require several paragraphs or pages. Lengthier arguments may require a Memorandum of Law. Check your local rules for formatting specifications and length restrictions.*)

4. *(Describe grounds for dismissal for lack of standing under 12(b)(1). See notation above in paragraph 3.)*

5. As a result of these deficiencies, plaintiff's complaint should be dismissed.

Respectfully submitted this ___ day of _____, 20__.

[Your signature and contact information]

CERTIFICATE OF SERVICE

I HEREBY CERTIFY that a true and correct copy of the foregoing has been served by the Notice of Electronic Filing, and was electronically filed with the Clerk of the Court via the CM/ECF system, which generates a notice of the filing to all attorneys of record, on this the ___ day of _____, 20__.

/s/ [your signature]

CHAPTER FOUR

The Clean Water Act

*Parsing Complex Regulatory Provisions
and Preparing a Citizen Suit*

ONE OF YOUR CLIENTS, Bobby Brown, owns property that abuts
the Keowee River, which is located entirely in South Carolina.
The Keowee originates at Lake Jocassee, a reservoir created by Lake
Jocassee Dam. The Keowee flows out of the reservoir for several
miles and eventually into Twelvemile Creek, which is the beginning
of the Seneca River. Twelvemile Creek and the Seneca River are also
located entirely in South Carolina. The Seneca River is a tributary of
the Savannah River, which crosses the South Carolina-Georgia border
before it empties into the Atlantic Ocean in Georgia. The portion of
the Keowee River that flows into Twelvemile Creek begins a stretch of
water, including the Seneca and Savannah Rivers, which is susceptible
for use to transport people or goods in interstate commerce. (See the
map provided on the next page.)

Ms. Brown recently called you to complain that she has noticed a
yellowish-brown tint to the water in the Keowee River running past
her property that she has never noticed in the five years she has lived
there. She asked you to investigate (1) whether the water is polluted; (2)
if so, whether it is dangerous for her and her family to swim or fish in
it; (3) if so, whether it is possible to identify the source of the pollution;
and, finally, (4) whether there is any way to stop further pollution of
the Keowee upstream from her property.

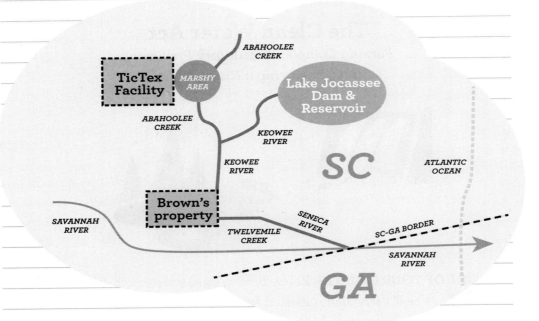

Because you are a partner in a firm that operates at a low profit margin, you decided to sample the water in the Keowee River near Brown's house yourself to determine if it is polluted. When you went to Brown's house, you noticed the same discoloration that she had. You filled a couple of mason jars with water from the River and took them to the local health department to see if the department could identify the presence of any chemicals in the water. After a few days, the health department informed you that the water contained a chemical called 2,6-Xylidine ("2,6-X"), which is used to make textile dyes and produces a yellow or brown tint when exposed to air or water.

After receiving this information, you called a college friend who works as a chemist for a chemical manufacturing company. Your friend told you that 2,6-X can irritate the skin upon contact, and can cause coughing, headaches, and dizziness when inhaled. In addition, 2,6-X has been classified as a possible human carcinogen by some international, federal, and state health agencies based on positive tests on laboratory animals.

To determine the possible source of 2,6-X in the Keowee River near your client's property, you looked at the federal Environmental Protection Agency (EPA)'s Toxic Release Inventory website, http://www2.epa.gov/toxics-release-inventory-tri-program. You searched for industrial facilities that use or produce chemicals subject to mandatory reporting duties under the Emergency Planning and Community Right-to-Know Act, 42 U.S.C. § 11023, and found that a company called TicTex, Inc. owns and operates a facility in South Carolina at which it dyes textiles for use in industrial processes. The Inventory indicates that TicTex handles chemical dyes, but does not specify which ones. After checking maps at the County Recording Office near Brown's home, you determined that the TicTex facility is located on property that contains a portion of a marshy area at a point northwest of, and about 3500 feet upgrade from, Abahoolee Creek. Abahoolee Creek runs into the Keowee River. The portion of the Creek between the marshy area and the Keowee River occasionally dries up in the late summer, but otherwise flows on a consistent basis into the Keowee River. Abahoolee Creek has never been used to transport goods in commerce and it would be impossible to do so in those summer months in which the Creek runs dry. It might be possible to use the Creek to transport goods when flow is relatively high, such as in the spring, but no one has ever tried. Commercial recreational outfitters have on occasion used the Creek as a site for guided canoeing trips for groups of both teenagers and adults.

Next, you checked public records maintained by the South Carolina Department of Health and Environmental Control (SCDHEC), which administers the Clean Water Act (CWA)'s National Pollutant Discharge Elimination System (NPDES) permit program for point sources located in the state. SCDHEC's public databases do not list TicTex as the holder of an NPDES permit. You have not been able to determine whether the TicTex plant uses or produces 2,6-X, but you know from publicly available information on the textile industry generally that the products TicTex makes and sells are treated with dyes containing 2,6-X at other textile manufacturing facilities in the United States. It is likely that if TicTex is discharging pollutants from its facility, it is emptying them into the marshy area.

After compiling the information described above, you arranged a meeting in your office with Ms. Brown. After you explained what you have discovered, you told her that it is possible that you could turn over the information to SCDHEC for further investigation and, if appropriate, enforcement action against TicTex. Brown replied that she has no knowledge of SCDHEC's track record in enforcing the CWA, but that she generally distrusts government agencies and would rather take things into her own hands (with your help) if that is possible. You told her that the CWA has a citizen suit mechanism, which allows any person to commence a civil action against any person "who is alleged to be in violation of . . . an effluent standard or limitation under [the CWA]." 33 U.S.C. § 1365(a)(1). Relevant portions of the CWA's citizen suit provisions are reproduced at the end of this chapter. Although the citizen suit provision does not allow federal courts to award compensatory damages to successful plaintiffs, they can impose civil penalties payable to the federal government and enjoin future violations.
You also explained that, as a condition for bringing a CWA citizen suit, a prospective plaintiff must notify the alleged violator at least 60 days before filing suit, and that if EPA or SCDHEC were to initiate and diligently prosecute an enforcement action against TicTex within that 60-day window of time, Brown's suit would be barred, although she could intervene if a civil suit were brought by EPA or SCDHEC in federal district court. Brown told you that she is willing to run the risk of her suit being barred, and that she would like you to explore the chances of her prevailing in a citizen suit against TicTex.

Points to Consider

After doing some additional research, you have identified several issues that are relevant to the chances of success in a citizen suit by Ms. Brown against TicTex and to whether you would be willing to file one on Brown's behalf.

Task 1. You need to determine whether, assuming that TicTex is dumping 2,6-X into the marshy area, its activities are subject to CWA jurisdiction. You know that EPA has addressed the scope of its regulatory jurisdiction under the CWA, and in particular, has interpreted the key statutory term "waters of the United States" in 40 C.F.R. § 122.2, which is provided at the end of this chapter. Unless TicTex is dumping 2,6-X or other pollutants into "waters of the United States," it is not required to obtain an NPDES permit. *See* 33 U.S.C. §§ 1311(a), 1362(7) & (12) (which are also provided at the end of this chapter). Analyze the regulations to determine if the marshy area qualifies as "waters of the United States," such that any discharge of 2,6-X into that area would require an NPDES permit. If you conclude that you lack sufficient information to make that determination, make a list of the factual questions you need to answer to make that determination.

Task 2. Assume for purposes of this question that you do not yet know if TicTex uses 2,6-X in its dying processes, has ever dumped 2,6-X into the marshy area near Abahoolee Creek, or is continuing to do so. You are concerned that if you bring a lawsuit on Brown's behalf based on what you do know, it may not be regarded as meritorious under Rule 3.1 of the Model Rules of Professional Responsibility. Assess whether you would be subject to sanctions for violating Rule 3.1 or Fed. R. Civ. P. 11 (provided in Appendix B of this book) if you brought a citizen suit against TicTex based on your current knowledge, with the intention of using discovery to unearth further information that would support the contention that TicTex has violated and is violating the CWA.

Task 3. Assuming for the purposes of this question that you can demonstrate that TicTex does use 2,6-X to dye its industrial textiles, you need to determine whether and when it has dumped that chemical into the marshy area and whether it is still doing so. You are concerned that if TicTex once dumped 2,6-X into waters of the United States upstream from Brown's property but is no longer doing so, the federal district court would lack subject matter jurisdiction over any citizen suit filed on behalf of Ms. Brown against TicTex or that such a suit may be dismissed as moot. How might you go about gathering the relevant information?

Task 4. Assume for purposes of this question that you conclude that TicTex has dumped and is continuing to dump 2,6-X into jurisdictional "waters of the United States." Based on your analysis of the first three points listed above, prepare a draft complaint in which you allege that TicTex is violating § 301(a) of the CWA, 33 U.S.C. § 1311(a), and request the issuance of an injunction preventing further illegal discharges. Examples of complaints can be found on www.uscourts.gov (check out the Illustrative Civil Rule Forms). Citizen suit complaints can be found on the websites of environmental public interest groups.

Task 5. In the event Brown's lawsuit is not foreclosed by enforcement actions initiated by EPA or SCDHEC and you are able to survive a motion to dismiss that you anticipate TicTex would file, you will need to muster evidence to support Brown's claim that TicTex is illegally discharging 2,6-X. TicTex can be expected to argue both that its activities are not subject to § 1311(a) and that, even if they are and they violate that provision, Brown has suffered no harm as a result. On the latter point, you would like to be able to introduce as evidence the water samples you collected that were analyzed by the local health department to show that Brown and her family have been and would be exposed to 2,6-X in using the Keowee River for recreational purposes. Would Rule 3.7 of the Model Rules of Professional Responsibility (provided in Appendix A of this book) preclude you from testifying as to the chain of custody of the water samples? If so, how could you overcome this problem?

Task 6. Like many citizen suit provisions, the CWA authorizes the award of litigation costs to a prevailing or substantially prevailing party. 33 U.S.C. § 1365(d). If you lose, however, you won't recover any fees or costs from the polluter. How might this influence your decision to proceed with a citizen suit? Do Rules 1.7 (conflict of interest) or 2.1 (advisor) of the Model Rules of Professional Responsibility have any bearing on your assessment?

> The Clean Water Act

CWA § 301, 33 U.S.C. § 1311. Effluent limitations

(a) Illegality of pollutant discharges except in compliance with law

Except as in compliance with this section and sections 1312, 1316, 1317, 1328, 1342, and 1344 of this title, the discharge of any pollutant by any person shall be unlawful.

. . .

CWA § 502, 33 U.S.C. § 1362. Definitions

Except as otherwise specifically provided, when used in [the CWA]:

. . .

(6) The term "pollutant" means dredged spoil, solid waste, incinerator residue, sewage, garbage, sewage sludge, munitions, chemical wastes, biological materials, radioactive materials, heat, wrecked or discarded equipment, rock, sand, cellar dirt and industrial, municipal, and agricultural waste discharged into water. This term does not mean (A) "sewage from vessels or a discharge incidental to the normal operation of a vessel of the Armed Forces" within the meaning of section 1322 of this title; or (B) water, gas, or other material which is injected into a well to facilitate production

of oil or gas, or water derived in association with oil or gas production and disposed of in a well, if the well used either to facilitate production or for disposal purposes is approved by authority of the State in which the well is located, and if such State determines that such injection or disposal will not result in the degradation of ground or surface water resources.

(7) The term "navigable waters" means the waters of the United States, including the territorial seas.

(8) The term "territorial seas" means the belt of the seas measured from the line of ordinary low water along that portion of the coast which is in direct contact with the open sea and the line marking the seaward limit of inland waters, and extending seaward a distance of three miles.

. . .

(12) The term "discharge of a pollutant" and the term "discharge of pollutants" each means (A) any addition of any pollutant to navigable waters from any point source, (B) any addition of any pollutant to the waters of the contiguous zone or the ocean from any point source other than a vessel or other floating craft.

. . .

(14) The term "point source" means any discernible, confined and discrete conveyance, including but not limited to any pipe, ditch, channel, tunnel, conduit, well, discrete fissure, container, rolling stock, concentrated animal feeding operation, or vessel or other floating craft, from which pollutants are or may be discharged. This term does not include agricultural stormwater discharges and return flows from irrigated agriculture.

. . .

CWA § 505, 33 U.S.C. § 1365. Citizen suits

(a) Authorization; jurisdiction

Except as provided in subsection (b) of this section and section 1319(g)(6) of this title, any citizen may commence a civil action on his own behalf—

(1) against any person (including (i) the United States, and (ii) any other governmental instrumentality or agency to the extent permitted by the eleventh amendment to the Constitution) who is alleged to be in violation of (A) an effluent standard or limitation under this chapter or (B) an order issued by the Administrator or a State with respect to such a standard or limitation . . . .

The district courts shall have jurisdiction, without regard to the amount in controversy or the citizenship of the parties, to enforce such an effluent standard or limitation, or such an order, or to order the Administrator to perform such act or duty, as the case may be, and to apply any appropriate civil penalties under section 1319(d) of this title.

(b) Notice

No action may be commenced—

(1) under subsection (a)(1) of this section—

(A) prior to sixty days after the plaintiff has given notice of the alleged violation (i) to the Administrator, (ii) to the State in which the alleged violation occurs, and (iii) to any alleged violator of the standard, limitation, or order, or

(B) if the Administrator or State has commenced and is diligently prosecuting a civil or criminal action in a court of the United States, or a State to require compliance with the standard, limitation, or order, but in any such action in a court of the United States any citizen may intervene as a matter of right. . . .

(d) Litigation costs

The court, in issuing any final order in any action brought pursuant to this section, may award costs of litigation (including reasonable attorney and expert witness fees) to any prevailing or substantially prevailing party, whenever the court determines such award is appropriate. . . .

(f) Effluent standard or limitation

For purposes of this section, the term "effluent standard or limitation under this chapter" means (1) effective July 1, 1973, an unlawful act under subsection (a) of section 1311 of this title; (2) an effluent limitation or other limitation under section

1311 or 1312 of this title; . . . [or] (6) a permit or condition thereof issued under section 1342 of this title; . . . .

(g) "Citizen" defined

For the purposes of this section the term "citizen" means a person or persons having an interest which is or may be adversely affected. . . .

> EPA's CWA Regulations Defining "Waters of the United States"

40 C.F.R. § 122.2. Waters of the United States or waters of the U.S. means:

(1) For purposes of the Clean Water Act, 33 U.S.C. 1251 et seq. and its implementing regulations, subject to the exclusions in paragraph (2) of this definition, the term "waters of the United States" means:

(i) All waters which are currently used, were used in the past, or may be susceptible to use in interstate or foreign commerce, including all waters which are subject to the ebb and flow of the tide;

(ii) All interstate waters, including interstate wetlands;

(iii) The territorial seas;

(iv) All impoundments of waters otherwise identified as waters of the United States under this section;

(v) All tributaries, as defined in paragraph (3)(iii) of this section, of waters identified in paragraphs (1)(i) through (iii) of this section;

(vi) All waters adjacent to a water identified in paragraphs (1)(i) through (v) of this definition, including wetlands, ponds, lakes, oxbows, impoundments, and similar waters;

. . .

(viii) All waters located within the 100–year floodplain of a water identified in paragraphs (1)(i) through (iii) of this definition and all waters located within 4,000 feet of the high tide line or ordinary high water mark of a water identified in paragraphs (1)(i) through (v) of this definition where they are determined on a case-specific basis to have a significant nexus to a water identified in paragraphs (1)(i) through (v) of this definition. For waters determined to have a significant nexus, the entire water is a water of the United States if a portion is located within the 100–year floodplain of a water identified in (1)(i) through (iii) of this definition or within 4,000 feet of the high tide line or ordinary high water mark. Waters identified in this paragraph shall not be combined with waters identified in paragraph (1)(vi) of this definition when performing a significant nexus analysis. If waters identified in this paragraph are also an adjacent water under paragraph (1)(vi), they are an adjacent water and no case-specific significant nexus analysis is required.

(2) The following are not "waters of the United States" even where they otherwise meet the terms of paragraphs (1)(iv) through (viii) of this definition.

. . .

(iv) The following features:

(A) Artificially irrigated areas that would revert to dry land should application of water to that area cease;

(B) Artificial, constructed lakes and ponds created in dry land such as farm and stock watering ponds, irrigation ponds, settling basins, fields flooded for rice growing, log cleaning ponds, or cooling ponds; . . .

(F) Erosional features, including gullies, rills, and other ephemeral features that do not meet the definition of tributary, non-wetland swales, and lawfully constructed grassed waterways; and

(G) Puddles.

(v) Groundwater, including groundwater drained through subsurface drainage systems.

. . .

(3) In this definition, the following terms apply:

(i) *Adjacent.* The term adjacent means bordering, contiguous, or neighboring a water identified in paragraphs (1)(i) through (v) of this definition, including waters separated by constructed dikes or barriers, natural river berms, beach dunes, and the like. For purposes of adjacency, an open water such as a pond or lake includes any wetlands within or abutting its ordinary high water mark. Adjacency is not limited to waters located laterally to a water identified in paragraphs (1)(i) through (v) of this definition. Adjacent waters also include all waters that connect segments of a water identified in paragraphs (1)(i) through (v) or are located at the head of a water identified in paragraphs (1)(i) through (v) of this definition and are bordering, contiguous, or neighboring such water. . . .

(ii) *Neighboring.* The term neighboring means:

(A) All waters located within 100 feet of the ordinary high water mark of a water identified in paragraphs (1)(i) through (v) of this definition. The entire water is neighboring if a portion is located within 100 feet of the ordinary high water mark;

(B) All waters located within the 100–year floodplain of a water identified in paragraphs (1)(i) through (v) of this definition and not more than 1,500 feet from the ordinary high water mark of such water. The entire water is neighboring if a portion is located within 1,500 feet of the ordinary high water mark and within the 100–year floodplain;

(C) All waters located within 1,500 feet of the high tide line of a water identified in paragraphs (1)(i) or (iii) of this definition, and all waters within 1,500 feet of the ordinary high water mark of the Great Lakes. The entire water is neighboring if a portion is located within 1,500 feet of the high tide line or within 1,500 feet of the ordinary high water mark of the Great Lakes.

(iii) *Tributary and tributaries.* The terms tributary and tributaries each mean a water that contributes flow, either directly or through another water (including an impoundment identified in paragraph (1)(iv) of this definition), to a water identified in paragraphs (1)(i) through (iii) of this definition that is characterized by the presence of the physical indicators of a bed and banks and an ordinary high water mark. These physical indicators demonstrate there is volume, frequency, and duration of flow sufficient to create a bed and banks and an ordinary high water mark, and thus to qualify as a tributary. A tributary can be a natural, man-altered, or man-made water and includes waters such as rivers, streams, canals, and ditches not excluded under paragraph (2) of this definition. A water that otherwise qualifies as a tributary under this definition does not lose its status as a tributary if, for any length, there are one or more constructed breaks (such as bridges, culverts, pipes, or dams), or one or more natural breaks (such as wetlands along the run of a stream, debris piles, boulder fields, or a stream that flows underground) so long as a bed and banks and an ordinary high water mark can be identified upstream of the break. A water that otherwise qualifies as a tributary under this definition does not lose its status as a tributary if it contributes flow through a water of the United States that does not meet the definition of tributary or through a non-jurisdictional water to a water identified in paragraphs (1)(i) through (iii) of this definition.

(iv) *Wetlands.* The term wetlands means those areas that are inundated or saturated by surface or groundwater at a frequency and duration sufficient to support, and that under normal circumstances do support, a prevalence of vegetation typically adapted for life in saturated soil conditions. Wetlands generally include swamps, marshes, bogs, and similar areas.

(v) *Significant nexus.* The term significant nexus means that a water, including wetlands, either alone or in combination with other similarly situated waters in the region, significantly affects the chemical, physical, or biological integrity of a water identified in paragraphs (1)(i) through (iii) of this definition. The term "in the region" means the watershed that drains to the nearest water identified in paragraphs (1)(i) through (iii) of this definition. For an effect to be significant, it must be more than speculative or insubstantial. Waters are similarly situated when they function alike and are sufficiently close to function together in affecting downstream waters. For purposes of determining whether or not a water has a significant nexus, the water's effect on downstream (1)(i) through (iii) waters shall be assessed by evaluating the aquatic functions identified in paragraphs (3)(v)(A) through (I) of this definition. A water has a significant nexus when any single function or combination of functions performed by the water, alone or together with similarly situated waters in the region, contributes significantly to the chemical, physical, or biological integrity of the nearest water identified in paragraphs (1)(i) through (iii) of this definition. Functions relevant to the significant nexus evaluation are the following:

(A) Sediment trapping,

(B) Nutrient recycling,

(C) Pollutant trapping, transformation, filtering, and transport,

(D) Retention and attenuation of flood waters,

(E) Runoff storage,

(F) Contribution of flow,

(G) Export of organic matter,

(H) Export of food resources, and

(I) Provision of life cycle dependent aquatic habitat (such as foraging, feeding, nesting, breeding, spawning, or use as a nursery area) for species located in a water identified in paragraphs (1)(i) through (iii) of this definition.

(vi) Ordinary high water mark. The term ordinary high water mark means that line on the shore established by the fluctuations of water and indicated by physical characteristics such as a clear, natural line impressed on the bank, shelving, changes in the character of soil, destruction of terrestrial vegetation, the presence of litter and debris, or other appropriate means that consider the characteristics of the surrounding areas. . . .

CHAPTER FIVE

The Comprehensive Environmental Response, Compensation, and Liability Act (CERCLA)

Minimizing CERCLA Liability Through Contribution Claims and Discovery

YOU ARE AN ASSOCIATE for a law firm with an environmental practice. The firm has just been retained by a new client, Recycling Saves Valuable Provisions, LLC (RSVP), which engages in various commercial recycling activities, to represent it in a matter involving the Comprehensive Environmental Response, Compensation, and Liability Act (CERCLA). RSVP has been named as a third-party defendant in a cost recovery action initially brought by the United States in federal district court in New Jersey against Stationary, Paper, and Ancillary Commodities, Inc. (SPAC) under §107(a) of CERCLA, 42 U.S.C. § 9607(a). Relevant portions of CERCLA are reproduced at the end of this chapter.

In its suit against SPAC, the United States alleged that it spent $100 million cleaning up a hazardous substance release at a leaking municipal landfill in Kearney, New Jersey. It sought reimbursement of its response costs from SPAC, which it argued was liable as a potentially responsible party (PRP) under § 107(a)(3). SPAC then brought RSVP into the case under § 113(f) of CERCLA, 42 U.S.C. § 9613(f), seeking contribution from RSVP for any liability imposed on SPAC to the United States. RSVP has hired your firm to defend it in SPAC's contribution action and to take whatever other steps it can to minimize RSVP's liability for cleanup costs at the landfill.

By reviewing the pleadings filed in the case, you have learned the following. After discovering that groundwater was contaminated with polychlorinated biphenyls (PCBs), the U.S. Environmental Protection Agency (EPA) determined that the source of the contamination was a leaking municipal solid waste landfill operated by the city of Kearney. The affected groundwater aquifer is hydrologically connected to a stream that runs into the Passaic River, which empties into Newark Bay. You know from prior experience working on environmental cases that PCBs are synthetic organic chemicals that were once used widely in the manufacture of refrigerants, paints, caulking and building materials, and paper products. The Toxic Substances Control Act, which Congress enacted in 1976, phased out and eventually banned the manufacture, distribution, and use of PCBs. *See* 15 U.S.C. § 2605(e). PCBs, which persist after entering the environment, may cause cancer in people who have been exposed to them over a long time. In addition, exposure to PCBs can cause anemia, damage to organs such as the liver and stomach, and disruption of the endocrine, immune, and reproductive systems in mammals, including humans. EPA hired contractors to excavate PCB-contaminated soils at the Kearney landfill and to treat contaminated groundwater at the site. EPA paid its contractors $100 million to perform these tasks.

The key to allocation of liability for EPA's cleanup expenses is determining how the PCBs found their way into the Kearney landfill. The pleadings provide partial answers to that question. Between 1951 and 1971, SPAC sold carbonless copy paper, which permitted a writer or typist to make instant copies of documents without the use of carbon paper. The back of a top sheet of paper was coated with an emulsion containing "microcapsules" of dye and solvent, which burst when a user wrote on the sheet, reproducing the same image on the lower sheet. A key ingredient of the emulsion was Arcilond, a PCB-based chemical solvent manufactured and sold by Priceless Industrial Chemicals Co. (PIC). SPAC purchased Arcilond from PIC and used it to manufacture its emulsion. SPAC sold the emulsion to Paterson

Paper Mills (PPM), which coated the paper and sold the finished carbonless paper products back to SPAC for commercial distribution. The government's complaint against SPAC alleges that between 1950, when PIC invented Arcilond, and 1971, SPAC purchased and used Arcilond in the manufacture of roughly 30 million pounds of emulsion, almost all of which it sold to PPM. PIC stopped selling products containing PCBs in 1970, and SPAC ceased using PCBs in its carbonless copy paper once it used up its stocks of Arcilond in 1971. After that, SPAC and other PIC customers began producing emulsion for use in making carbonless copy paper using a chemical manufactured by PIC that did not contain PCBs.

PCBs used to make carbonless copy paper ended up in the Kearney landfill because some of the emulsion that PPM used to coat the paper that it later sold to SPAC was excess material that it could not reuse in its coating process. After mixing that waste with its other industrial waste, PPM transported all of its industrial waste for disposal at the Kearney landfill. SPAC's third-party compliant alleged that waste sent to the landfill by your client, RSVP, contained additional amounts of PCBs.

RSVP has verified that SPAC's allegation is true. The client's production manager has explained to you the relevant portion of its business. Producing paper from raw materials is expensive. The production process creates material called "broke," which is composed of waste, scraps, and undersized paper rolls that are unusable by the original manufacturer. Making paper from recycled broke is cheaper than making it from scratch. RSVP purchased broke from other paper mills through middlemen and used it to make paper. It also purchased broke from PPM. Upon receipt of the broke, RSVP separated the usable fibers in the broke from the coating, thus removing the PCBs from the portion of the paper that went into the new product. Between 1955 and 1967, RSVP sent its waste, including the PCBs, for disposal at the Kearney landfill.

You believe that an important factor in the allocation of liability for the government's cleanup costs at the Kearney landfill is when those involved in the manufacture and use of products containing PCBs knew of its toxic properties. You have done some preliminary research on that question, including contacting researchers at the Centers for Disease Control (CDC) in Atlanta. The CDC researchers told you that some European governments suspected as early as 1962 or 1963 that human exposure to PCBs was problematic. Peer-reviewed published studies on tests on laboratory mice conducted at that time showed a correlation between exposure to PCBs and both immune system impairment and an abnormally high incidence of liver tumors. Based on a tip provided by the CDC researchers, you contacted a long-time plant manager at English Stationary Products Co. (ESP), a paper manufacturing company which has operated in England since the 1950s. The plant manager told you that, although it was before he began working for ESP, the scuttlebutt among ESP employees is that ESP used to purchase Arcilond from PIC to manufacture carbonless copy paper using a process very similar to the one used by SPAC. Further, rumor has it that ESP stopped buying Arcilond from PIC in 1963 precisely because it was aware of the research showing the pos-sible dangers of exposure to PCBs and was afraid of incurring either tort or regulatory liability if it kept using Arcilond to manufacture paper. The ESP employee did not know whether ESP explained these concerns to anyone at PIC when it decided not to renew its Arcilond purchase contract with PIC upon its expiration. But the employee indicated that it is common practice in the industry for product manufacturers to inquire about the reasons that their customers have decided to switch suppliers or discontinue using products previously covered by long-term contracts. Besides, the ESP employee indicated that part of the responsibilities of its own scientists is to keep track of scientific studies worldwide that might affect the company's production processes or the marketability of its products, and he assumes this is standard practice within the chemical manufacturing industry, too.

 ## Points to Consider

Task 1. RSVP's goal is to minimize its liability in the cost recovery litigation concerning the Kearney landfill. Does RSVP have a plausible defense that would shield it from any CERCLA liability, based either on rebutting SPAC's prima facie case or on an affirmative defense?

Task 2. As another strategy for minimizing the scope of RSVP's liability in the event it is held to be a liable PRP, your firm wants you to consider filing third-party claims for contribution against PIC and PPM pursuant to § 113(f) of CERCLA. Based on your knowledge of CERCLA, you anticipate that if you bring PIC into the litigation, it will argue it is not liable because all it did was sell a useful product (Arcilond) for use in the production of carbonless paper, another useful product. As a result, PIC did not arrange for the disposal of hazardous substances so as to trigger liability under § 107(a)(3) of CERCLA. Based on your reading of the case law concerning arranger liability under CERCLA, do you think this defense is likely to succeed?

Task 3. Assume you have filed contribution claims against PIC and PPM as PRPs. You understand that the battle over liability will be resolved by the district court's application of "appropriate" equitable factors under § 113(f)(1)'s third sentence. Your task now is to draft interrogatories that will elicit information useful to RSVP in pursuing its contribution claims against the two PRPs that RSVP brought into the case. Based on the case law governing the resolution of contribution actions under § 113(f), provided below, and on Rules 26 and 33 of the Federal Rules of Civil Procedure, reproduced in Appendix B of this book, draft interrogatories that may be served on PIC and PPM during discovery. You should also draft a list of questions to be directed at your own client so that you have the information necessary to advocate on behalf of your client in the contribution litigation.

Task 4. After you brought PIC into the case, it filed a third-party complaint asserting a contribution action against the city of Kearney, which it asserts is liable as the owner and operator of the landfill that was the subject of EPA's response action. Your firm has long represented the city in a host of matters, including but not limited to environmental matters. The firm has never represented the city in a CERCLA case, however, and the city has not (yet) asked the firm to represent it in the pending CERCLA suit. Does your firm's ongoing representation of the city pose conflict of interest problems for the firm? Consider Rules 1.7 and 1.8 of the Model Rules of Professional Conduct, which are included in Appendix A. If you think there is a conflict, how would you go about resolving it? Must the firm withdraw from representing RSVP in the CERCLA litigation?

> The Comprehensive Environmental Response, Compensation, and Liability Act

CERLA § 107, 42 U.S.C. § 9607. Liability

(a) Covered persons; scope; recoverable costs and damages . . .

Notwithstanding any other provision or rule of law, and subject only to the defenses set forth in subsection (b) of this section—

(1) the owner and operator of a vessel or a facility,

(2) any person who at the time of disposal of any hazardous substance owned or operated any facility at which such hazardous substances were disposed of,

(3) any person who by contract, agreement, or otherwise arranged for disposal or treatment, or arranged with a transporter for transport for disposal or treatment, of hazardous substances owned or possessed by such person, by any other party or entity, at any facility or incineration vessel owned or operated by another party or entity and containing such hazardous substances, and

(4) any person who accepts or accepted any hazardous substances for transport to disposal or treatment facilities, incineration vessels or sites selected by such person,

from which there is a release, or a threatened release which causes the incurrence of response costs, of a hazardous substance, shall be liable for—

(A) all costs of removal or remedial action incurred by the United States Government or a State or an Indian tribe not inconsistent with the national contingency plan;

. . . .

(b) Defenses

There shall be no liability under subsection (a) of this section for a person otherwise liable who can establish by a preponderance of the evidence that the release or threat of release of a hazardous substance and the damages resulting therefrom were caused solely by—

(1) an act of God;

(2) an act of war;

(3) an act or omission of a third party other than an employee or agent of the defendant, or than one whose act or omission occurs in connection with a contractual relationship, existing directly or indirectly, with the defendant (except where the sole contractual arrangement arises from a published tariff and acceptance for carriage by a common carrier by rail), if the defendant establishes

by a preponderance of the evidence that (a) he exercised due care with respect to the hazardous substance concerned, taking into consideration the characteristics of such hazardous substance, in light of all relevant facts and circumstances, and (b) he took precautions against foreseeable acts or omissions of any such third party and the consequences that could foreseeably result from such acts or omissions; or

(4) any combination of the foregoing paragraphs.

* * *

CERCLA § 113, 42 U.S.C. § 9613. Civil proceedings

. . .

(f) Contribution

(1) Any person may seek contribution from any other person who is liable or potentially liable under section 107(a) of this title, during or following any civil action under section 106 of this title or under section 107(a) of this title. Such claims shall be brought in accordance with this section and the Federal Rules of Civil Procedure, and shall be governed by Federal law. In resolving contribution claims, the court may allocate response costs among liable parties using such equitable factors as the court determines are appropriate. . . .

CHAPTER SIX

The Resource Conservation and Recovery Act (RCRA)

Assessing Whether a Material is a Solid Waste and Defending Against a Citizen Suit

THE LAW FIRM for which you work as an associate represents Total Adhesive Production Engineering, Inc. (TAPE), a manufacturer of products that include adhesives, paint removers, and typewriter correction fluids. One of the chemicals that TAPE has used in the past in the manufacture of these products is trichloroethylene (TCE), which is widely used as an industrial solvent, such as a degreasing agent for metal parts and as a solvent in dry cleaning processes. In the past few years, TAPE has begun substituting a chemical called n-propyl bromidine (NPB) for TCE as a material input in its production processes. It has done so primarily because the U.S. Environmental Protection Agency (EPA) has discouraged the use of TCE due to the potential adverse health effects upon exposed individuals, including damage to the nervous system, Parkinson's disease, and cancer. EPA has indicated that it is considering banning further production and use of TCE under the Toxic Substances Control Act. Seeing the handwriting on the wall, TAPE decided to substitute NPB for TCE as a feedstock in its production processes. Medical research indicates that exposure to NPB may create neurological problems, but at doses somewhat higher than the doses of TCE that create similar health risks. In addition, while EPA upgraded TCE in 2011 from a possible to a known human carcinogen, the agency has classified NPB as a chemical for which inadequate information exists to assess its carcinogenic potential.

Another reason that TAPE has substituted NPB for TCE as an input is that its manufacturing processes generate a form of NPB as a chemical intermediate. A chemical intermediate is a chemical substance produced during the conversion of some reactant to a product. Substances generated by one step in a production process and used for the succeeding step are considered intermediates. TAPE  is therefore able to use the NPB generated by its production processes as a raw material instead of purchasing NPB from suppliers, saving it considerable amounts of money. The NPB generated by TAPE's production processes, however, has higher concentrations of hazardous constituents than those found in commercially available NPB.

The Resource Conservation and Recovery Act (RCRA) is the federal statute that governs solid and hazardous waste management. Under RCRA, a solid waste (as defined in § 1004(27)) with concentrations of certain hazardous constituents above amounts designated by EPA in its regulations qualifies as a hazardous waste (as defined in § 1004(5)) because it exhibits one of the four characteristics of a hazardous waste (toxicity). *See, e.g.,* 40 C.F.R. § 261.24 (providing that a solid waste exhibits the characteristic of toxicity, rendering it a hazardous waste, if "the extract from a representative sample of the waste contains any of the contaminants listed in table 1 at the concentration equal to or greater than the respective value given in that table"). Even newly manufactured NPB exhibits the toxicity characteristic, but the NPB generated by TAPE's processes contains considerably higher concentrations of the relevant hazardous constituents.

In order to make the NPB generated by TAPE usable as a feedstock in its production processes, TAPE entered into a "tolling agreement" with Manufacturers Associated Guaranteed Industrial Conversion (MAGIC). A tolling agreement is a contract in which one party agrees for a fee to convert an input supplied to it by another party into a product that can then be used by the input supplier in its business. Under this agreement, TAPE delivers the "contaminated" NPB generated in its manufacturing processes to MAGIC, which treats the NPB, resulting in a reduction of its hazardous constituents to a level consistent with the levels that are typically found in newly manufactured, "virgin" NPB. When the treatment process is complete, TAPE picks up the processed NPB and returns it to its plant to be used in the manufacture of adhesives, paint removers, and typewriter correction fluids. Even after paying the tolling fee, it is cheaper for TAPE to use the treated NPB than it would be to purchase virgin NPB.

Recently, you met with Alexander Anderson, TAPE's Chief Operating Officer, at his office at the plant, which is located in Pasacagoula, Mississippi. Anderson told you that he had some concerns about the implementation of TAPE's tolling agreement with MAGIC. According to Anderson, the version of NPB produced by TAPE has sufficiently high concentrations of hazardous constituents that he is concerned that TAPE's workers, particularly those responsible for putting the NPB in drums and preparing them for shipping to MAGIC, may face health risks because of their exposure. Anderson told you that he has no firm scientific evidence that plant workers are at risk, but a few workers have complained to the on-site nurse of headaches. Before TAPE began trying to reprocess NPB for further use in its production processes, there were no such complaints. Anderson also said the company is in the process of doing research into the availability of respirators that plant workers handling NPB could use to minimize NPB inhalation, but until those respirators are used in the plant, there is no way to know how effective they will be. In addition, Anderson expressed concern that sometimes the barrels of NPB that are scheduled to be shipped to MAGIC sit on TAPE's outdoor loading dock for several weeks, where they are exposed to the elements. Because TAPE's plant is located near the Gulf Coast, it is exposed to hurricane activity, which could result in movement or rupturing of the barrels awaiting transport. Anderson said that he has urged the company's President to accelerate the schedule for transport of the NPB barrels so that they are sitting at the loading dock for less time. The President told Anderson he would look into the problem, but so far nothing has been done. Anderson asked you to consider whether any of TAPE's current practices violate applicable federal, state, or local environmental requirements. He also pleaded with you not to repeat these conversations with anyone except other attorneys at your firm, and especially not to contact TAPE's President, because Anderson does not want the President to think he is either a "tree hugger" or a prophet of doom. Anderson also expressed concern that if information about management of the materials covered by the TAPE contract went public before TAPE had settled on a strategy for how to minimize health and environmental risks (or the likely perception of them), EPA might charge it with RCRA violations before TAPE has a chance to correct them and, even if it doesn't, the company's image could be tarnished.

 ## Initial Points to Consider

Task 1. Based on what you learned at your meeting with Anderson, do you have an ethical obligation to inform EPA, state environmental regulators, the local health department, or the plant's workers about the health and environmental risks associated with implementation of the MAGIC tolling agreement, or is that protected confidential information? Consider Rules 1.6 and 1.13 of the Model Rules of Professional Conduct (provided in Appendix A of this book).

Additional Points to Consider

Yesterday, you received another phone call from Anderson. This time, he was in full panic mode. He told you that he just received a letter from a local citizens group, Pascagoulans Livid About Irresponsible Deliveries (PLAID), notifying TAPE that PLAID intends to file a citizen suit against it if EPA does not begin diligent prosecution of its own enforcement action against TAPE within 90 days. According to the letter, PLAID intends to file an action under § 7002(a)(1)(B) of RCRA, 42 U.S.C. § 6972(a)(1)(B) (reproduced below), to enjoin TAPE from continuing to manage solid waste in a manner that contributes to an imminent and substantial endangerment to health and the environment. The letter indicated that PLAID members noticed that barrels stacked up on TAPE's loading dock sometimes remain there for weeks, creating a risk of damage and leakage during severe weather. The members also noticed a skull and crossbones label taped to each barrel, leading them to believe the barrels contain dangerously toxic materials. Finally, the letter indicated that PLAID members have followed the trucks that transport TAPE's barrels to the MAGIC plant in nearby Gulfport, Mississippi and it asserts that the route includes roads in poor condition that create a significant risk of accidents, which may result in spills of the barrels' contents, with resulting harm to the public health and the environment.

Anderson pleaded with you to figure out a way to defend the citizen suit, if PLAID brings it after waiting the required 90 days specified in § 7002(b)(2)(A).

Task 2. Anderson has consulted with TAPE's President and Board of Directors about the letter from PLAID. Although he did not mention to them his previous concerns about confidentiality, it is clear that "the cat is out of the bag," at least about the loading dock problem, because a prerequisite to filing a RCRA citizen suit is providing the same 90-day notice to EPA as PLAID has provided to TAPE. See 42 U.S.C. § 6972(a)(2)(A)(i). (Assume for purposes of this problem that EPA, not Mississippi, administers RCRA's hazardous waste management program in the state.) At the meeting with the President and the Board, Anderson recommended three strategies. One is to contact EPA to see if it will bring an administrative enforcement action against TAPE under § 3008 of RCRA, 42 U.S.C. § 6928, which the parties can then settle, hopefully on terms favorable to TAPE. Such a government enforcement action would preclude PLAID from pursuing its citizen suit under § 7002(b)(2)(B). The second strategy is to seek to defeat any actions brought against it by either EPA or PLAID by arguing that the NPB covered by TAPE's tolling agreement with MAGIC is not solid waste, and therefore is not covered by RCRA. The third strategy is to seek a non-waste determination under § 260.34 of EPA's RCRA regulations.

a) The Board's preference is to follow the second strategy because, if successful, it negates the possibility of any liability for violations of RCRA. Based on the provisions of RCRA and EPA implementing regulations reproduced below, assess the likelihood that TAPE could convince a court that the NPB does not qualify as solid waste (and therefore as a hazardous waste, either).

b) The Board was amenable to the third strategy as well because, if successful, it will avoid the need to comply with the hazardous waste management provisions adopted pursuant to Subtitle C of RCRA, although by the time TAPE receives an answer to its submission under § 260.34 from EPA, PLAID likely will already have filed its citizen suit (unless it is blocked by EPA's diligent prosecution). Based on your reading of EPA's RCRA regulations, what are the chances of convincing EPA to issue a non-waste determination for the NPB?

c) Assume for purposes of this question only that your analysis convinces you that the NPB likely qualifies as solid waste. You have arranged a meeting with EPA's regional office to try to convince it to file an administrative action against TAPE that would block PLAID's citizen suit. Be prepared to make arguments and offers at a negotiating session with EPA attorneys so that TAPE may successfully pursue the first strategy.

Task 3. Assume for purposes of this question that EPA chose not to file an enforcement action against TAPE, at least at this time. PLAID filed its citizen suit against TAPE, alleging that TAPE's NPB-related activities are contributing to an imminent and substantial endangerment to public health and the environment. PLAID seeks a permanent injunction preventing further implementation of the MAGIC tolling agreement until TAPE has presented the court with a fully developed, adequate plan to reduce the risks posed by TAPE's current practices. In the interim, PLAID has sought a preliminary injunction pursuant to Rule 65 of the Federal Rules of Civil Procedure (provided in Appendix B of this book), to immediately halt implementation of the tolling agreement pending the court's resolution of the case on the merits.

PLAID's motion for a preliminary injunction alleges that the careless storage of NPB-laden barrels at TAPE's loading dock, its use of inadequate containers to ship the NPB to and from MAGIC's plant (which TAPE reuses after emptying the treated NPB for use in its production process), and the transportation of the NPB on deteriorated roadways create substantial risks of accidents, leaks, and spills. Further, PLAID alleges that its members live in close proximity either to TAPE's loading dock or along the route TAPE uses to transport the NPB barrels to and from MAGIC's plant. As a result, if spills or leaks occur, PLAID's members will be exposed to the escaped NPB, creating irreparable harm in the form of heightened risks of contracting illnesses associated with NPB exposure, including irreversible neurological damage and cancer.

The partner in your firm that heads up the environmental practice has asked you to prepare an opposition to PLAID's motion for a preliminary injunction. Draft such a response, using the facts currently at your disposal and identifying any additional information you should seek from TAPE to bolster your arguments. Anderson has told you that if the court were to halt further implementation of the MAGIC tolling agreement, even on a temporary basis, TAPE's production processes would necessarily grind to a halt, requiring severe cost-cutting measures, including the likelihood of laying off about half of the company's fifty production line employees. For several examples of briefs opposing preliminary injunctions in environmental cases, *see Grace Christian Fellowship v. KJG Investments*, Inc., 2008 WL 5370222 (E.D. Wis.), filed in 2008; *Sierra Club v. Gates*, 2007 WL 2066146 (S.D. Ind.), filed in 2007; and *San Luis & Delta-Mendota Water Auth. v. Jewell,* http://earthjustice.org/sites/default/files/files/TrinityTROoppositionPCFFA8-13-13.pdf (opposition to motion for temporary restraining order), filed in 2013.

> The Resource Conservation and Recovery Act

RCRA § 1004, 42 U.S.C. § 6903.

. . .

(3) The term "disposal" means the discharge, deposit, injection, dumping, spilling, leaking, or placing of any solid waste or hazardous waste into or on any land or water so that such solid waste or hazardous waste or any constituent thereof may enter the environment or be emitted into the air or discharged into any waters, including ground waters.

. . .

(5) The term "hazardous waste" means a solid waste, or combination of solid wastes, which because of its quantity, concentration, or physical, chemical, or infectious characteristics may—

(A) cause, or significantly contribute to an increase in mortality or an increase in serious irreversible, or incapacitating reversible, illness; or

(B) pose a substantial present or potential hazard to human health or the environment when improperly treated, stored, transported, or disposed of, or otherwise managed.

. . .

(27) The term "solid waste" means any garbage, refuse, sludge from a waste treatment plant, water supply treatment plant, or air pollution control facility and other discarded material, including solid, liquid, semisolid, or contained gaseous material resulting from industrial, commercial, mining, and agricultural operations, and from community activities . . . .

. . .

(33) The term "storage", when used in connection with hazardous waste, means the containment of hazardous waste, either on a temporary basis or for a period of years, in such a manner as not to constitute disposal of such hazardous waste.

. . .

> EPA Regulations

40 C.F.R. Part 260
Hazardous Waste Management System: General

§ 260.10. Definitions

. . .

Contained means held in a unit . . . that meets the following criteria:

(1) The unit is in good condition, with no leaks or other continuing or intermittent unpermitted releases of the hazardous secondary materials to the environment, and is designed, as appropriate for the hazardous secondary materials, to prevent releases of hazardous secondary materials to the environment. Unpermitted releases are releases that are not covered by a permit (such as a permit to discharge to water or air) and may include, but are not limited to, releases through surface transport by precipitation runoff, releases to soil and groundwater, wind-blown dust, fugitive air emissions, and catastrophic unit failures;

. . .

(3) The unit holds hazardous secondary materials that are compatible with other hazardous secondary materials placed in the unit and is compatible with the materials used to construct the unit and addresses any potential risks of fires or explosions.

. . .

Disposal means the discharge, deposit, injection, dumping, spilling, leaking, or placing of any solid waste or hazardous waste into or on any land or water so that such solid waste or hazardous waste or any constituent thereof may enter the environment or be emitted into the air or discharged into any waters, including ground waters.

. . .

Hazardous secondary material means a secondary material (e.g., spent material, by-product, or sludge) that, when discarded, would be identified as hazardous waste under part 261 of this chapter.

. . .

Management or hazardous waste management means the systematic control of the collection, source separation, storage, transportation, processing, treatment, recovery, and disposal of hazardous waste.

. . .

Storage means the holding of hazardous waste for a temporary period, at the end of which the hazardous waste is treated, disposed of, or stored elsewhere.

§ 260.30. Non-waste determinations and variances from classification as a solid waste

In accordance with the standards and criteria in § 260.31 and § 260.34 and the procedures in § 260.33, the Administrator may determine on a case-by-case basis that the following recycled materials are not solid wastes:

. . .

(b) Materials that are reclaimed and then reused within the original production process in which they were generated;

(c) Materials that have been reclaimed but must be reclaimed further before the materials are completely recovered; [and]

. . .

(e) Hazardous secondary materials that are indistinguishable in all relevant aspects from a product or intermediate.

. . .

§ 260.33. Procedures for variances from classification as a solid waste, for variances to be classified as a boiler, or for non-waste determinations

The Administrator will use the following procedures in evaluating applications for variances from classification as a solid waste, applications to classify particular enclosed controlled flame combustion devices as boilers, or applications for non-waste determinations.

(a) The applicant must apply to the Administrator for the variance or non-waste determination. The application must address the relevant criteria contained in § 260.31, § 260.32, or § 260.34, as applicable.

. . .

§ 260.34. Standards and criteria for non-waste determinations

(a) An applicant may apply to the Administrator for a formal determination that a hazardous secondary material is not discarded and therefore not a solid waste. The determinations will be based on the criteria contained in paragraphs (b) or (c) of this section, as applicable. If an application is denied, the hazardous secondary material might still be eligible for a solid waste variance or exclusion (for example, one of the solid waste variances under § 260.31).

. . .

(c) The Administrator may grant a non-waste determination for hazardous secondary material which is indistinguishable in all relevant aspects from a product or intermediate if the applicant demonstrates that the hazardous secondary material is comparable to a product or intermediate and is not discarded. The determination will be based on whether the hazardous secondary material is legitimately recycled as specified in § 260.43 and on the following criteria:

(1) Whether market participants treat the hazardous secondary material as a product or intermediate rather than a waste (for example, based on the current positive value of the hazardous secondary material, stability of demand, or any contractual arrangements);

(2) Whether the chemical and physical identity of the hazardous secondary material is comparable to commercial products or intermediates;

(3) Whether the capacity of the market would use the hazardous secondary material in a reasonable time frame and ensure that the hazardous secondary material will not be abandoned (for example, based on past practices, market factors, the nature of the hazardous secondary material, or any contractual arrangements);

(4) Whether the hazardous constituents in the hazardous secondary material are reclaimed rather than released to the air, water or land at significantly higher levels from either a statistical or from a health and environmental risk perspective than would otherwise be released by the production process; and

(5) Other relevant factors that demonstrate the hazardous secondary material is not discarded, including why the hazardous secondary material cannot meet, or should not have to meet, the conditions of an exclusion under § 261.2 or § 261.4 of this chapter.

§ 260.43. Legitimate recycling of hazardous secondary materials

(a) Recycling of hazardous secondary materials for the purpose of the exclusions or exemptions from the hazardous waste regulations must be legitimate. Hazardous secondary material that is not legitimately recycled is discarded material and is a solid waste. In determining if their recycling is legitimate, persons must address all the requirements of this paragraph.

(1) Legitimate recycling must involve a hazardous secondary material that provides a useful contribution to the recycling process or to a product or intermediate of the recycling process. The hazardous secondary material provides a useful contribution if it:

(i) Contributes valuable ingredients to a product or intermediate; or

(ii) Replaces a catalyst or carrier in the recycling process; or

(iii) Is the source of a valuable constituent recovered in the recycling process; or

(iv) Is recovered or regenerated by the recycling process; or

(v) Is used as an effective substitute for a commercial product.

(2) The recycling process must produce a valuable product or intermediate. The product or intermediate is valuable if it is:

(i) Sold to a third party; or

(ii) Used by the recycler or the generator as an effective substitute for a commercial product or as an ingredient or intermediate in an industrial process.

(3) The generator and the recycler must manage the hazardous secondary material as a valuable commodity when it is under their control. Where there is an analogous raw material, the hazardous secondary material must be managed, at a minimum, in a manner consistent with the management of the raw material or in an equally protective manner. Where there is no analogous raw material, the hazardous secondary material must be contained. Hazardous secondary materials that are released to the environment and are not recovered immediately are discarded.

(4) The product of the recycling process must be comparable to a legitimate product or intermediate:

(i) Where there is an analogous product or intermediate, the product of the recycling process is comparable to a legitimate product or intermediate if:

(A) The product of the recycling process does not exhibit a hazardous characteristic (as defined in part 261 subpart C) that analogous products do not exhibit, and

(B) The concentrations of any hazardous constituents found in appendix VIII of part 261 of this chapter that are in the product or intermediate are at levels that are comparable to or lower than those found in analogous products or at levels that meet widely-recognized commodity standards and specifications, in the case where the commodity standards and specifications include levels that specifically address those hazardous constituents. . . .

. . .

(iii) If the product of the recycling process has levels of hazardous constituents that are not comparable to or unable to be compared to a legitimate product or intermediate per paragraph (a)(4)(i) or (ii) of this section, the recycling still may be shown to be legitimate, if it meets the following specified requirements. The person performing the recycling must conduct the necessary assessment and prepare documentation showing why the recycling is, in fact, still legitimate. The recycling can be shown to be legitimate based on lack of exposure from toxics in the product, lack of the bioavailability of the toxics in the product, or other relevant considerations which show that the recycled product does not contain levels of hazardous constituents that pose a significant human health or environmental risk.

40 C.F.R. Part 261
Identification and Listing of Hazardous Waste

§ 261.1. Purpose and scope

(a) This part identifies those solid wastes which are subject to regulation as hazardous wastes under parts 262 through 265, 268 [of RCRA]. . . .

(b)(1) The definition of solid waste contained in this part applies only to wastes that also are hazardous for purposes of the regulations implementing subtitle C of RCRA. For example, it does not apply to materials (such as non-hazardous scrap, paper, textiles, or rubber) that are not otherwise hazardous wastes and that are recycled.

. . .

(c) For the purposes of §§ 261.2 and 261.6:

(1) A "spent material" is any material that has been used and as a result of contamination can no longer serve the purpose for which it was produced without processing;

. . .

(3) A "by-product" is a material that is not one of the primary products of a production process and is not solely or separately produced by the production process. Examples are process residues such as slags or distillation column bottoms. The term does not include a co-product that is produced for the general public's use and is ordinarily used in the form it is produced by the process.

(4) A material is "reclaimed" if it is processed to recover a usable product, or if it is regenerated. Examples are recovery of lead values from spent batteries and regeneration of spent solvents. In addition, for purposes of § 261.4(a)(23) and (24), smelting, melting, and refining furnaces are considered to be solely engaged in metals reclamation if the metal recovery from the hazardous secondary materials meets the same requirements as those specified for metals recovery from hazardous waste found in § 266.100(d)(1) through (3) of this chapter, and if the residuals meet the requirements specified in § 266.112 of this chapter.

(5) A material is "used or reused" if it is either:

(i) Employed as an ingredient (including use as an intermediate) in an industrial process to make a product (for example, distillation bottoms from one process used as feedstock in another process). However, a material will not satisfy this condition if distinct components of the material are recovered as separate end products (as when metals are recovered from metal-containing secondary materials); or

(ii) Employed in a particular function or application as an effective substitute for a commercial product (for example, spent pickle liquor used as phosphorous precipitant and sludge conditioner in wastewater treatment).

. . .

(7) A material is "recycled" if it is used, reused, or reclaimed.

§ 261.2 Definition of solid waste

(a)(1) A solid waste is any discarded material that is not excluded under § 261.4(a) or that is not excluded by a variance granted under §§ 260.30 and 260.31 or that is not excluded by a non-waste determination under §§ 260.30 and 260.34.

(2)(i) A discarded material is any material which is:

. . .

(B) Recycled, as explained in paragraph (c) of this section; . . .

(c) Materials are solid wastes if they are recycled—or accumulated, stored, or treated before recycling—as specified in paragraphs (c)(1) through (4) of this section.

. . .

(3) Reclaimed. Materials noted with a "-" in column 3 of Table 1 are not solid wastes when reclaimed. Materials noted with an "*" in column 3 of Table 1 are solid wastes when reclaimed unless they meet the requirements of §§ 261.4(a) (17), or 261.4(a)(23), 261.4(a)(24), or 261.4(a)(27).[1]

. . .

(e) Materials that are not solid waste when recycled.

(1) Materials are not solid wastes when they can be shown to be recycled by being:

(i) Used or reused as ingredients in an industrial process to make a product, provided the materials are not being reclaimed; or

(ii) Used or reused as effective substitutes for commercial products . . .

---

1 Both "Spent materials" and "By-products exhibiting a characteristic of hazardous waste" are marked with an * in Table 1.

(g) Sham recycling. A hazardous secondary material found to be sham recycled is considered discarded and a solid waste. Sham recycling is recycling that is not legitimate recycling as defined in § 260.43.

§ 261.4. Exclusions

(a) Materials which are not solid wastes. The following materials are not solid wastes for the purpose of this part:

. . .

(23) Hazardous secondary material generated and legitimately reclaimed within the United States or its territories and under the control of the generator, provided that the material complies with paragraphs (a)(23)(i) and (ii) of this section:

. . .

(i)(C) The hazardous secondary material is generated pursuant to a written contract between a tolling contractor and a toll manufacturer and is reclaimed by the tolling contractor, if the tolling contractor certifies the following: "On behalf of [insert tolling contractor name], I certify that [insert tolling contractor name] has a written contract with [insert toll manufacturer name] to manufacture [insert name of product or intermediate] which is made from specified unused materials, and that [insert tolling contractor name] will reclaim the hazardous secondary materials generated during this manufacture. On behalf of [insert tolling contractor name], I also certify that [insert tolling contractor name] retains ownership of, and responsibility for, the hazardous secondary materials that are generated during the course of the manufacture, including any releases of hazardous secondary materials that occur during the manufacturing process." . . . For purposes of this paragraph, tolling contractor means a person who arranges for the production of a product or intermediate made from specified unused materials through a written contract with a toll manufacturer. Toll manufacturer means a person who produces a product or intermediate made from specified unused materials pursuant to a written contract with a tolling contractor.

(ii)(A) The hazardous secondary material is contained as defined in § 260.10 of this chapter. A hazardous secondary material released to the environment is discarded and a solid waste unless it is immediately recovered for the purpose of reclamation. Hazardous secondary material managed in a unit with leaks or other continuing or intermittent unpermitted releases is discarded and a solid waste. . . .

CHAPTER SEVEN

The Clean Air Act

Challenging the Adequacy of a State's
New Source Review Program

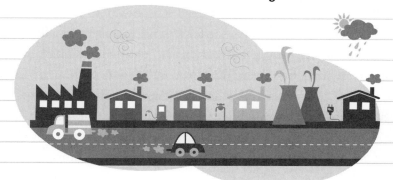

SECTION 109(b) OF THE CLEAN AIR ACT (CAA), 42 U.S.C.
§ 7409(b), authorizes EPA to establish primary and secondary national ambient air quality standards (NAAQS) that are requisite to protect the public health, allowing an adequate margin of safety, and the public welfare. EPA has adopted NAAQS for six air pollutants, known as criteria pollutants, including ozone, lead, particulate matter, oxides of nitrogen, sulfur dioxide, and carbon monoxide. Section 110(a) of the CAA requires states to adopt and submit for EPA review a separate state implementation plan (SIP) for each criteria pollutant for which EPA has adopted NAAQS. If a state's SIP meets mandatory statutory requirements, EPA must approve it. 42 U.S.C. § 7410(k)(3). If a SIP fails to satisfy federal requirements, EPA must afford states the opportunity to correct deficiencies identified by EPA and, if the state fails to revise its SIP to conform to those requirements, EPA may issue a federal implementation plan for the state. 42 U.S.C. § 7410(c).

Section 110(a)(2) contains the list of statutory requirements that all SIPs must meet. One of these requirements is that the SIP include "a program to provide for . . . regulation of the modification and construction of any stationary sources within the areas covered by the plan as necessary to assure that [the NAAQS] are achieved, including a permit program as required in parts C and D of [the CAA]." 42 U.S.C. § 7410(a)(2)(C). Part C is a reference to the Prevention of Significant Deterioration (PSD) provisions of the CAA, which govern areas of the country that have air quality better than what is required by the NAAQS. These areas are known as "clean air areas" or PSD areas. Every state that includes PSD areas for a particular criteria pollutant must establish a program that prohibits the commencement of construction of any major emitting facility in a PSD area without a PSD permit. Section 165(a) describes the conditions under which a state may issue such a construction permit. 42 U.S.C. § 7475(a). Part D of the CAA includes the provisions governing areas of the country that have not yet achieved the NAAQS, which are known as nonattainment areas. 42 U.S.C. § 7501(4). States containing nonattainment areas must revise their SIPs to meet the mandatory requirements listed in § 172(c), 42 U.S.C. § 7502(c). One of those requirements is that the SIP "require permits for the construction and operation of new or modified major stationary sources located anywhere in the nonattainment area." 42 U.S.C. § 7502(c)(5). Section 173, 42 U.S.C. § 7503, sets forth the substantive requirements for issuance of a nonattainment permit area permit. Together, the permit requirements stemming from §§ 110(a)(2)(C), 165(a), and 172(c)(5) are known as New Source Review (NSR). Relevant CAA provisions are reproduced at the end of this chapter.

In May of last year, the Arizona Department of Environmental Quality (ADEQ) submitted for EPA's approval under the CAA revisions to the provisions of its state implementation plans that govern the CAA's NSR programs for all criteria pollutants. EPA published a notice of proposed rulemaking in the Federal Register in which it proposed to approval Arizona's revised NSR SIP provisions and solicited public comment. The following January, EPA issued final regulations approving the state's revised SIPs.

You are an attorney for a regional non-profit environmental public interest group, Arizona Citizens for Clean Air (ACCA). You have worked for ACCA for several years. Before joining ACCA, you worked in the Office of General Counsel at EPA. During your tenure at EPA, you provided advice to EPA's Office of Air and Radiation (OAR), which is responsible for administering the CAA, on whether regulations it drafted complied with the agency's responsibilities under the CAA. You also participated in meetings at which the Administrator discussed strategies for the adoption and implementation of such rules. Some of these meetings included discussion of how to ensure that states met their duties to adopt adequate SIPs.

ACCA's Board of Directors asked the organization's legal team to review EPA's approval of Arizona's SIP revisions to determine if the approval is consistent with the requirements of the CAA and EPA implementing regulations. The team, of which you are a part, has identified several problems with the approval.

1. Your team believes that ADEQ did not comply with statutory and regulatory requirements dictating the procedures for adopting SIPs and SIP revisions. The state provided notice of its proposed SIP revisions and solicited written comments from interested members of the public. ACCA submitted comments identifying the substantive defects in the proposed revisions described below. ADEQ also held a hearing on the proposal. While interested members of the public could attend, no member of the public was allowed to make an oral presentation. Instead, ADEQ officials discussed the agency's rationale for the proposed SIP revisions. At the end of the hearing, an ADEQ official invited those present to submit additional written comments if they disagreed with any of ADEQ's reasoning or positions. Your team thinks that this set of procedures did not comply with either § 110(l) of the CAA (reproduced below) or

EPA's regulations, 40 C.F.R. § 51.102 (also reproduced below), because EPA failed to allow oral presentations at the hearing on its proposed SIP revisions.

2. Your team objects to a provision of ADEQ's SIPs, as approved by EPA, that allows either a proposed new major emitting facility to be located in a PSD area or a proposed new major stationary source to be located in a nonattainment area to commence construction after ADEQ's issuance of a "proposed final permit." In its notice of proposed rulemaking considering whether to approve ADEQ's SIP revisions, EPA identified this provision of the SIPs as a violation of §§ 165(a), 172(c)(5), and § 51.160 of EPA's NSR regulations (reproduced below). When EPA finally approved the plans, however, it concluded that this provision of Arizona's SIPs does not violate either the CAA or § 51.160. In response to EPA's proposed rejection of this provision of the SIPs, ADEQ explained that it used the term "proposed final permit" to address the fact that the state has created a "unitary" NSR permit program, rather than the "binary" program adopted in most other states. Binary programs require separate permits for commencement of construction and operation. Under such a program, a source covered by NSR may commence construction immediately after it receives a construction permit but may not begin operating until the agency has issued an operating permit after inspecting the plant to ensure that it is capable of complying with applicable NSR requirements. Under a unitary program, a covered source receives a single consolidated construction and operating permit. The "proposed final permit" allows the source to commence construction, even though it may not commence operating until it receives the final permit. ADEQ explained that it adopted this approach to avoid subjecting sources subject to NSR to regulatory burdens (delays in commencement of construction) that similar sources in states with binary programs do not face.

ADEQ also explained that it adopted a provision in an agency manual that prohibits ADEQ air regulators from allowing commencement of construction until after the issuance of a proposed final permit, and that a proposed final permit is, despite its name, tantamount to a final agency action subject to judicial review in state court immediately upon issuance. ACCA believes that the manual provisions are not enforceable, as some state court decisions have held, and that judicial review of the state's issuance of a proposed final permit may not be available because, as its name implies, it is not a final agency decision. Therefore, a source subject to NSR can commence construction and no one can challenge the state's approval of such commencement until the issuance of a final permit. By that time, the source will have sunk so much money into the project that a court will be reluctant to enjoin operation even if it is ultimately determined that the permit violates CAA requirements.

3. Your team believes that the Arizona SIPs are defective because they do not include the term "subject to regulation," which appears in § 165(a)(4) and which is defined in § 51.166(b)(48) of EPA's regulations (reproduced below). Rather, the SIPs require all PSD permit recipients to be subject to the best available control technology for all pollutants regulated as criteria pollutants. Greenhouse gases that contribute to climate change are not criteria pollutants and EPA has not issued NAAQS for them. Your team thinks the SIPs' NSR provisions for both the PSD and nonattainment component of NSR are too narrow, and that EPA should have rejected the SIP revision due to its failure to (a) require sources in PSD areas that are covered by NSR to achieve emissions limitations for greenhouse gases that reflect the best available control technology; or (b) require sources in nonattainment areas that are covered by NSR to achieve emission limitations for greenhouse gases that reflect the lowest achievable emission rate.

Points to Consider

Task 1. ACCA has decided to petition the Court of Appeals for the Ninth Circuit for review of EPA's final regulations approving Arizona's SIP revisions on the three grounds described above. You are concerned, however, that, as a former attorney in EPA's Office of General Counsel, you may have a conflict of interest that precludes you from representing ACCA in this matter. When you worked at EPA, you advised EPA's OAR on the provisions it should include in its NSR regulations, including the ones which you believe Arizona's SIP violates. Considering Rules 1.9 and 1.11 of the Model Rules of Professional Responsibility, which are reproduced in Appendix A, should you recuse yourself from participating in ACCA's challenge? If you decide that you are unable to work on this matter, how will that affect ACCA's ability to pursue its challenge to EPA's approval of Arizona's SIP revisions?

Task 2. Assume you decide that you are able to work on ACCA's challenge to EPA's approval of the Arizona SIP revisions. Consider the three substantive grounds described above on which you might challenge EPA's action as a violation of the CAA or EPA's implementing regulations. Based on your analysis, advise ACCA's Board of Directors whether all three challenges are viable and which ones have the greatest chance of succeeding.

Task 3. Based on the advice you provided to the Board, draft a petition for review of EPA's approval of the Arizona SIP revisions that you may file in the Ninth Circuit pursuant to § 307(b)(1) of the CAA (reproduced below). You should look at Rule 15 of the Federal Rules of Appellate Procedure (reproduced below) and the model petition for review in the Appellate Rules Forms provided by the federal courts (reproduced below), which is also available at http://www.ca9.uscourts.

gov/forms/ (Form 3). Note that experienced attorneys and students alike use forms as checklists when drafting their own motions and petitions to ensure that they've covered all the pertinent bases and have not neglected any relevant possibilities. Forms can be a trap for the unwary, though; be careful when using them, and be sure to analyze every provision carefully and revise it as necessary to ensure that it fits your situation.

You also may want to watch a video available on the 9th Circuit's website about appellate practice before that court. *See United States Court of Appeals for the Ninth Circuit, Perfecting Your Appeal: A Simple Guide for the Proper and Timely Preparation of Your Appeal*, http://www.ca9.uscourts.gov/guides/perfecting_your_appeal.php. Finally, for examples of petitions for judicial review challenging EPA actions under the CAA and CWA, see http://www.chamberlitigation.com/sites/default/files/U.S.%20Chamber,%20et%20al.%20v.%20EPA%20(ESPS)%20—%20Petition%20for%20Review.pdf; http://waterkeeper.org/cms/assets/uploads/2015/07/WKA-et.-al-v.-U.S.-EPA-et-al-9th-Cir.-Petition-for-Review-7.22.15.pdf.

> The Clean Air Act

CAA § 110, 42 U.S.C. § 7410. State implementation plans for national primary and secondary ambient air quality standards

(a) Adoption of plan by State; submission to Administrator; content of plan; revision; new sources; indirect source review program; supplemental or intermittent control systems

(1) Each State shall, after reasonable notice and public hearings, adopt and submit to the Administrator, within 3 years (or such shorter period as the Administrator may prescribe) after the promulgation of a national primary ambient air quality standard (or any revision thereof) under section 109 of this title for any air pollutant, a plan which provides for implementation, maintenance, and enforcement of such primary standard in each air quality control region (or portion thereof) within such State. . . .

(2) Each implementation plan submitted by a State under this chapter shall be adopted by the State after reasonable notice and public hearing. Each such plan shall—

(A) include enforceable emission limitations and other control measures, means, or techniques . . . , as well as schedules and timetables for compliance, as may be necessary or appropriate to meet the applicable requirements of this chapter;

. . .

(C) include a program to provide for the enforcement of the measures described in subparagraph (A), and regulation of the modification and construction of any stationary source within the areas covered by the plan as necessary to assure that national ambient air quality standards are achieved, including a permit program as required in parts C and D of this subchapter;

. . .

(k) Environmental Protection Agency action on plan submissions

. . .

(3) . . . In the case of any submittal on which the Administrator is required to act under paragraph (2), the Administrator shall approve such submittal as a whole if it meets all of the applicable requirements of this chapter. . . . The plan revision shall not be treated as meeting the requirements of this chapter until the Administrator approves the entire plan revision as complying with the applicable requirements of this chapter.

. . .

(l) Plan revisions

Each revision to an implementation plan submitted by a State under this chapter shall be adopted by such State after reasonable notice and public hearing. The Administrator shall not approve a revision of a plan if the revision would interfere with any . . . applicable requirement of this chapter.

. . .

CAA § 165, 42 U.S.C. § 7475. Preconstruction requirements

(a) Major emitting facilities on which construction is commenced

No major emitting facility on which construction is commenced after August 7, 1977, may be constructed in any area to which this part applies unless—

(1) a permit has been issued for such proposed facility in accordance with this part setting forth emission limitations for such facility which conform to the requirements of this part;

. . .

(4) the proposed facility is subject to the best available control technology for each pollutant subject to regulation under this chapter emitted from, or which results from, such facility; . . .

. . .

CAA § 179, 42 U.S.C. § 7479. Definitions

For purposes of [the PSD provisions:

. . .

(3) The term "best available control technology" means an emission limitation based on the maximum degree of reduction of each pollutant subject to regulation under this chapter emitted from or which results from any major emitting facility, which the permitting authority, on a case-by-case basis, taking into account energy, environmental, and economic impacts and other costs, determines is achievable for such facility . . . .

CAA § 171, 42 U.S.C. § 7501. Definitions

For purposes of [the nonattainment provisions]:

. . .

(3) The term "lowest achievable emission rate" means for any source, that rate of emissions which reflects—

(A) the most stringent emission limitation which is contained in the implementation plan of any State for such class or category of source, unless the owner or operator of the proposed source demonstrates that such limitations are not achievable, or

(B) the most stringent emission limitation which is achieved in practice by such class or category of source, whichever is more stringent.

In no event shall the application of this term permit a proposed new or modified source to emit any pollutant in excess of the amount allowable under applicable new source standards of performance.

. . .

CAA § 172, 42 U.S.C. § 7502. Nonattainment plan provisions in general

(c) Nonattainment plan provisions—The plan provisions (including plan items) required to be submitted under this part shall comply with each of the following:

. . .

(5) Permits for new and modified major stationary sources

Such plan provisions shall require permits for the construction and operation of new or modified major stationary sources anywhere in the nonattainment area, in accordance with section 7503 of this title.

. . .

CAA § 173, 42 U.S.C. § 7503. Permit requirements

(a) In general—The permit program required by [§ 172(c)(5)] shall provide that permits to construct and operate may be issued if—

. . .

(2) the proposed source is required to comply with the lowest achievable emission rate . . . .

CAA § 502, 42 U.S.C. § 7602. Definitions

. . .

(j) Except as otherwise expressly provided, the terms "major stationary source" and "major emitting facility" mean any stationary facility or source of air pollutants which directly emits, or has the potential to emit, one hundred tons per year or more of any air pollutant (including any major emitting facility or source of fugitive emissions of any such pollutant, as determined by rule by the Administrator).

. . .

CAA § 307, 42 U.S.C. § 7607. Administrative proceedings and judicial review

(b)(1) A petition for review of the Administrator's action in approving or promulgating any implementation plan under section 7410 of this title or section 7411(d) of this title, . . . or under regulations thereunder, . . . or any other final action of the Administrator under this chapter . . . which is locally or regionally applicable may be filed only in the United States Court of Appeals for the appropriate circuit. . . .

> EPA's Clean Air Act Regulations

40 C.F.R. § 51.102 Public hearings

(a) Except as otherwise provided in paragraph (c) of this section and within the 30 day notification period as required by paragraph (d) of this section, States must provide notice, provide the opportunity to submit written comments and allow the public the opportunity to request a public hearing. The State must hold a public hearing or provide the public the opportunity to request a public hearing. The notice announcing the 30 day notification period must include the date, place and time of the public hearing. If the State provides the public the opportunity to request a public hearing and a request is received the State must hold the scheduled hearing or schedule a public hearing (as required by paragraph (d) of this section). . . . These requirements apply for adoption and submission to EPA of:

(1) Any plan or revision of it . . . .

. . .

(e) The State must prepare and retain, for inspection by the Administrator upon request, a record of each hearing. The record must contain, as a minimum, a list of witnesses together with the text of each presentation.

(f) The State must submit with the plan, revision, or schedule, a certification that the requirements in paragraph (a) and (d) of this section were met. Such certification will include the date and place of any public hearing(s) held or that no public hearing was requested during the 30 day notification period.

(g) Upon written application by a State agency (through the appropriate Regional Office), the Administrator may approve State procedures for public hearings. The following criteria apply:

(1) Procedures approved under this section shall be deemed to satisfy the requirement of this part regarding public hearings.

(2) Procedures different from this part may be approved if they—

(i) Ensure public participation in matters for which hearings are required; and

(ii) Provide adequate public notification of the opportunity to participate.

(2) The Administrator may impose any conditions on approval he or she deems necessary.

40 C.F.R. § 51.160 Legally enforceable procedures

(a) Each plan must set forth legally enforceable procedures that enable the State or local agency to determine whether the construction or modification of a facility, building, structure or installation, or combination of these will result in—

(1) A violation of applicable portions of the control strategy; or

(2) Interference with attainment or maintenance of a national standard in the State in which the proposed source (or modification) is located or in a neighboring State.

(b) Such procedures must include means by which the State or local agency responsible for final decisionmaking on an application for approval to construct or modify will prevent such construction or modification if—

(1) It will result in a violation of applicable portions of the control strategy; or

(2) It will interfere with the attainment or maintenance of a national standard.

. . .

40 C.F.R. § 51.166(b) Definitions

All State plans shall use the following definitions for the purposes of this section. Deviations from the following wording will be approved only if the State specifically demonstrates that the submitted definition is more stringent, or at least as stringent, in all respects as the corresponding definitions below:

. . .

(48) Subject to regulation means, for any air pollutant, that the pollutant is subject to either a provision in the Clean Air Act, or a nationally-applicable regulation codified by the Administrator in subchapter C of this chapter, that requires actual control of the quantity of emissions of that pollutant, and that such a control requirement has taken effect and is operative to control, limit or restrict the quantity of emissions of that pollutant released from the regulated activity. Except that:

(i) Greenhouse gases (GHGs), the air pollutant defined in § 86.1818–12(a) of this chapter as the aggregate group of six greenhouse gases: Carbon dioxide, nitrous oxide, methane, hydrofluorocarbons, perfluorocarbons, and sulfur hexafluoride, shall not be subject to regulation except as provided in paragraph (b)(48)(iv) . . . of this section.

. . .

(iv) Beginning January 2, 2011, the pollutant GHGs is subject to regulation if:

(a) The stationary source is a new major stationary source for a regulated NSR pollutant that is not GHGs, and also will emit or will have the potential to emit 75,000 tpy CO2e or more . . .

. . . .

> Federal Rules of Appellate Procedure Rule 15, 28 U.S.C.A.

Rule 15. Review or Enforcement of an Agency Order— How Obtained; Intervention

(a) Petition for Review; Joint Petition.

(1) Review of an agency order is commenced by filing, within the time prescribed by law, a petition for review with the clerk of a court of appeals authorized to review the agency order. . . .

(2) The petition must:

(A) name each party seeking review either in the caption or the body of the petition—using such terms as "et al.," "petitioners," or "respondents" does not effectively name the parties;

(B) name the agency as a respondent (even though not named in the petition, the United States is a respondent if required by statute); and

(C) specify the order or part thereof to be reviewed.

(3) Form 3 in the Appendix of Forms is a suggested form of a petition for review.

(4) In this rule "agency" includes an agency, board, commission, or officer; "petition for review" includes a petition to enjoin, suspend, modify, or otherwise review, or a notice of appeal, whichever form is indicated by the applicable statute.

(b) Application or Cross-Application to Enforce an Order; Answer; Default.

(1) An application to enforce an agency order must be filed with the clerk of a court of appeals authorized to enforce the order. If a petition is filed to review an agency order that the court may enforce, a party opposing the petition may file a cross-application for enforcement.

(2) Within 21 days after the application for enforcement is filed, the respondent must serve on the applicant an answer to the application and file it with the clerk. If the respondent fails to answer in time, the court will enter judgment for the relief requested.

(3) The application must contain a concise statement of the proceedings in which the order was entered, the facts upon which venue is based, and the relief requested.

(c) Service of the Petition or Application. The circuit clerk must serve a copy of the petition for review, or an application or cross-application to enforce an agency order, on each respondent as prescribed by Rule 3(d), unless a different manner of service is prescribed by statute. At the time of filing, the petitioner must:

(1) serve, or have served, a copy on each party admitted to participate in the agency proceedings, except for the respondents;

(2) file with the clerk a list of those so served; and

(3) give the clerk enough copies of the petition or application to serve each respondent.

. . .

(e) Payment of Fees. When filing any separate or joint petition for review in a court of appeals, the petitioner must pay the circuit clerk all required fees.

FEDERAL RULES OF APPELLATE PROCEDURE
FORM 3, 28 U.S.C.A.

Form 3. Petition for Review of Order of an Agency,
Board, Commission or Officer

United States Court of Appeals for the _____ Circuit

A.B.,	)	
Petitioner	)	PETITION FOR
v.	)	REVIEW
	)	
XYZ Commission,	)	
Respondent	)	

[(here name all parties bringing the petition[1])] hereby petitions the court for review of the Order of the XYZ Commission (describe the order) entered on _____ , 20 ___.

[(s)]
_____
Attorney for Petitioners

Address:
_____

_____

_____

---

1   See Rule 15.

CHAPTER EIGHT

Criminal Enforcement
Exercising Prosecutorial Discretion

YOU ARE A NEW Assistant U.S. Attorney. Your neighbor, Alexander Anderson, recently approached you about a possible criminal case arising out of activities at Total Adhesive Production Engineering, Inc. (TAPE), a manufacturer of adhesives, paint removers, correction fluids, and related products. As described further in Chapter 6, TAPE produces, reclaims, and uses a chemical called n-propyl bromidine (NPB) in its production processes. As part of the reclamation process, employees must handle and repackage drums of NPB, which sit on TAPE's outdoor loading dock for several weeks before being picked up by another company for reprocessing.

Medical research indicates that exposure to NPB may create neuro-logical problems in high doses, but the U.S. EPA has classified NPB as a chemical for which inadequate information exists to assess its carcinogenic potential. The version of NPB produced by TAPE has sufficiently high concentrations of hazardous constituents that Anderson, formerly TAPE's Chief Operating Officer, has long been concerned that TAPE's workers, particularly those responsible for putting the NPB in drums and preparing them for reclamation, face significant health risks.

Anderson told you a few workers have complained to the on-site nurse of headaches. He also told you that he had discussed his concerns with the President of the company, Dennis Drago. When Anderson assured Drago that he had no firm scientific evidence that plant workers were at risk of serious or long-lasting health effects, Drago told him that he would hire a consultant to look into the potential risks and possible protective measures for plant workers to minimize their exposure to NPB.

According to Anderson, the consultant, Connie Caution, informed Drago and Anderson about several new studies regarding the health effects of NPB. According to the National Institute for Occupational Safety and Health (NIOSH), workplace exposure can cause irritation of the eyes, lungs, and skin and can damage the nervous system. Initial neurologic effects appear as headaches and dizziness. If workers are exposed to high concentrations over longer periods of time, they are likely to experience slurred speech, confusion, difficulty walking, muscle twitching, and loss of feeling in their arms and legs. The risk to workers depends on the concentration of NPB in the air 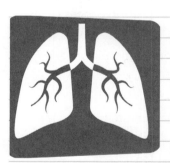 they breathe, how much comes in contact with skin, and length of exposure. In addition, animal studies suggest that NPB exposure may result in reduced blood cell counts and immunosuppression along with toxicity to the liver and to the reproductive and neurologic systems. Based on these and other recent studies, the National Toxicology Program administered by the Department of Health and Human Services has classified NPB as a human carcinogen. This has prompted EPA to consider changing NPB's status for its own regulatory purposes as well. Caution advised Drago to take immediate action to either stop using NPB or to bring in an industrial hygienist to implement exposure-preventing measures such as respirators and protective clothing.

After Caution signed a confidentiality agreement, Drago thanked Caution for her information, paid for her services, and told her that they needed no further assistance at this time. Later, in a closed door session, Drago told Anderson that under no circumstances should Caution's advice be leaked to the employees or anyone else, because TAPE was in the process of negotiating a lucrative sales agreement with 3M, a multinational conglomerate, and Drago feared that bad press would cause 3M to back out. Until EPA required them to do something different, Drago said, it would be business as usual.

Anderson, in dismay, decided to take an early retirement. He came to you after he heard what happened to Sally Silkwood, a neighbor and long-time employee of TAPE. Silkwood was one of several employees responsible for packaging the NPB and preparing it for reclamation. In the course of the past year, Silkwood had seen the plant's nurse several times about headaches, nausea, and dizziness. The nurse gave her Tylenol and advised her to take some of her sick leave and go home and relax. Silkwood took some time off. When she returned to work after a few days, she asked to be moved to a different position, but was told she'd need to wait until something suitable opened up. About six months 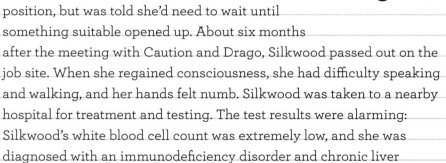 after the meeting with Caution and Drago, Silkwood passed out on the job site. When she regained consciousness, she had difficulty speaking and walking, and her hands felt numb. Silkwood was taken to a nearby hospital for treatment and testing. The test results were alarming: Silkwood's white blood cell count was extremely low, and she was diagnosed with an immunodeficiency disorder and chronic liver failure. She will need a liver transplant and long-term care.

Assume for purposes of this chapter that the NPB produced and reclaimed at TAPE is a hazardous waste under the

Resource Conservation and Recovery Act (RCRA) (an issue that was the subject of Chapter 6). TAPE did not have a RCRA permit for NPB, but it was in the process of obtaining one when Anderson retired. Anderson supervised the personnel who filled out the applications and, upon completion, submitted them to Drago for his perusal. Just before Anderson retired, Drago instructed him to revise the application to report reduced quantities and concentrations of NPB used at the plant even though no such reductions had occurred. Anderson did as he was told, but he refused to sign the application. Drago signed it himself and his assistant submitted it to EPA.

 ## Points to Consider

Task 1. Should you prosecute TAPE? If so, what counts should you include? Write a concise charging memo to your boss, the U.S. Attorney. Consider whether you will be likely to prove every element of each criminal charge, given the higher burden of proof applicable to criminal actions. Relevant provisions of RCRA are provided below.

In addition to the legal issues, be sure to consider the policy implications of your recommendation. The U.S. Department of Justice's guidance on environmental criminal prosecutions lists several specific factors for your consideration, including the violator's voluntary disclosure, cooperation, and any preventative measures and compliance programs. U.S. DOJ, Factors in Decisions on Criminal Prosecutions for Environmental Violations, http://www.justice.gov/enrd/selected-publications/factors-decisions-criminal-prosecutions (July 1991, updated Apr. 15, 2015). The guidance lists additional factors and provides examples. Also, in recent years, the Department has prioritized the prosecution of corporate crime and, in particular, cases where employees are endangered by workplace conditions. U.S. DOJ, Worker Endangerment, http://www.justice.gov/enrd/worker-endangerment (May 6, 2015);

U.S. DOJ, U.S. Attorney's Manual, Principles of Federal Prosecution of Business Organizations § 9-28.010, available at http://www.justice.gov/usam/usam-9-28000-principles-federal-prosecution-business-organizations#9-28.500.

You will wish to confer with EPA staff as well; their perspectives and expertise on hazardous waste permitting will be invaluable. For information about EPA's enforcement priorities and outcomes, see U.S. EPA, National Enforcement Priorities, http://www.epa.gov/enforcement/national-enforcement-initiatives (Oct. 15, 2015) (established on three-year cycles); U.S. EPA, Criminal Enforcement Overview (Aug. 12, 2015), http://www.epa.gov/enforcement/criminal-enforcement-overview; and U.S. EPA, 2014 Major Criminal Cases, http://www.epa.gov/enforcement/2014-major-criminal-cases (Dec. 18, 2014).

Task 2. Should you prosecute Drago individually? In *United States v. Dotterweich*, 320 U.S. 277 (1943), the U.S. Supreme Court held that responsible corporate officers could be held personally and criminally liable for violating strict liability statutes protecting the public welfare. Consider the merits of such a prosecution under RCRA, and whether the goals of environmental enforcement would be advanced by it. As you are weighing your options, consider Model Rule 3.1 regarding the lawyer's duty to advance meritorious claims and contentions. You should also take note of Rule 3.8 regarding the special responsibilities of a prosecutor. Both Rules are provided in Appendix A of this book.

Task 3. It took courage for a "whistleblower" like Anderson to approach you. It will take at least as much courage for Silkwood and Caution to cooperate with the prosecution. If you proceed, you'll likely need all of them to testify. What might you tell them to alleviate their concerns about the personal consequences to them of testifying against TAPE or Drago and to make them comfortable sharing information with you?

Task 4. Assume that you've gone forward with a prosecution, and Drago's attorney wants to discuss a plea bargain with you. On behalf of both TAPE and himself, Drago would agree to implement state-of-the-art environmental compliance systems and worker safety protocols at a cost of up to of $150,000. In exchange, Drago wants all charges dropped and a press release issued from your office describing the new environmentally- and worker-friendly initiatives and TAPE's restored status as a good corporate citizen. Make a recommendation to the U.S. Attorney.

> The Resource Conservation and Recovery Act (RCRA)

42 U.S.C. § 6903. Definitions

* * *

(15) The term "person" means an individual, trust, firm, joint stock company, corporation (including a government corporation), partnership, association, State, municipality, commission, political subdivision of a State, or any interstate body and shall include each department, agency, and instrumentality of the United States. . . .

42 U.S.C. 6928(d). Federal Enforcement

(d) Any person who . . .

(2) knowingly treats, stores, or disposes of any hazardous waste . . . without a permit . . . ;

(3) knowingly omits material information or makes any false material statement or representation in any application, label, manifest, record, report, permit, or other document filed, maintained, or used for purposes of compliance with regulations

promulgated by the Administrator (or by a State in the case of an authorized State program) under this subchapter; [or]

(4) knowingly generates, stores, treats, transports, disposes of, exports, or otherwise handles any hazardous waste or any used oil not identified or listed as a hazardous waste under this subchapter . . . and who knowingly destroys, alters, conceals, or fails to file any record, application, manifest, report, or other document required to be maintained or filed for purposes of compliance with regulations promulgated by the Administrator (or by a State in the case of an authorized State program) under this subchapter. . . .

shall, upon conviction, be subject to a fine of not more than $50,000 for each day of violation, or imprisonment not to exceed two years (five years in the case of a violation of paragraph . . . (2)), or both. . . .

(e) Any person who knowingly transports, treats, stores, disposes of, or exports any hazardous waste . . . in violation of . . . subsection (d) of this section who knows at that time that he thereby places another person in imminent danger of death or serious bodily injury, shall, upon conviction, be subject to a fine of not more than $250,000 or imprisonment for not more than fifteen years, or both. A defendant that is an organization shall, upon conviction of violating this subsection, be subject to a fine of not more than $1,000,000.

(f) For the purposes of subsection (e) of this section—

(1) A person's state of mind is knowing with respect to—

(A) his conduct, if he is aware of the nature of his conduct;

(B) an existing circumstance, if he is aware or believes that the circumstance exists; or

(C) a result of his conduct, if he is aware or believes that his conduct is substantially certain to cause danger of death or serious bodily injury.

(2) In determining whether a defendant who is a natural person knew that his conduct placed another person in imminent danger of death or serious bodily injury—

(A) the person is responsible only for actual awareness or actual belief that he possessed; and

(B) knowledge possessed by a person other than the defendant but not by the defendant himself may not be attributed to the defendant;

Provided, That in proving the defendant's possession of actual knowledge, circumstantial evidence may be used, including evidence that the defendant took affirmative steps to shield himself from relevant information.

(3) It is an affirmative defense to a prosecution that the conduct charged was consented to by the person endangered and that the danger and conduct charged were reasonably foreseeable hazards of—

(A) an occupation, a business, or a profession; or

(B) medical treatment or medical or scientific experimentation conducted by professionally approved methods and such other person had been made aware of the risks involved prior to giving consent.

The defendant may establish an affirmative defense under this subsection by a preponderance of the evidence. . . .

(5) The term "organization" means a legal entity, other than a government, established, or organized for any purpose, and such term includes a corporation, company, association, firm, partnership, joint stock company, foundation, institution, trust, society, union, or any other association of persons.

(6) The term "serious bodily injury" means—

(A) bodily injury which involves a substantial risk of death;

(B) unconsciousness;

(C) extreme physical pain;

(D) protracted and obvious disfigurement; or

(E) protracted loss or impairment of the function of a bodily member, organ, or mental faculty.

42 U.S.C. § 6971. Employee Protection

(a) General—No person shall fire, or in any other way discriminate against, or cause to be fired or discriminated against, any employee or any authorized representative of employees by reason of the fact that such employee or representative has filed, instituted, or caused to be filed or instituted any proceeding under this chapter or under any applicable implementation plan, or has testified or is about to testify in any proceeding resulting from the administration or enforcement of the provisions of this chapter. . . .

(b) Remedy—Any employee or a representative of employees who believes that he has been fired or otherwise discriminated against by any person in violation of subsection (a) of this section may, within thirty days after such alleged violation occurs, apply to the Secretary of Labor for a review of such firing or alleged discrimination. . . . Upon receipt of such application, the Secretary of Labor shall cause such investigation to be made as he deems appropriate. . . . Upon receiving the report of such investigation, the Secretary of Labor shall make findings of fact. If he finds that such violation did occur, he shall issue a decision, incorporating an order therein and his findings, requiring the party committing such violation to take such affirmative action to abate the violation as the Secretary of Labor deems appropriate, including, but not limited to, the rehiring or reinstatement of the employee or representative of employees to his former position with compensation. If he finds that there was no such violation, he shall issue an order denying the application. . . .

CHAPTER NINE

Toxic Torts

Making FOIA and Discovery Requests; Working with Experts

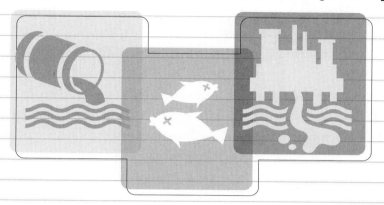

YOUR CLIENT, Penny Peterson, owns a 640-acre cattle ranch that abuts the Western River, near Gunsmoke, New Mexico. During the mid-1990s, Summit Corp. owned and operated the Gold Summit Mine, an underground mine located about 30 miles upstream from Penny's ranch. Over the years, Gold Summit Mine produced a half-million ounces of gold and two million ounces of silver. In 1999, Summit Corp. shifted its focus to the production of high-tech alloys from mines in Brazil and closed the Gold Summit Mine. Since then, it has been looking for a purchaser for the mine, to no avail. Summit reached an agreement with the U.S. EPA and the state of New Mexico on a plan to close the site, including capping the mine to prevent acid mine drainage from old mining shafts from spilling into the Western River.

When Summit crews began working on the closure last July, they underestimated how much water had collected at the mine site. When their backhoe shifted a temporary "plug," basically a large pile of dirt (or "backfill") heaped at the mouth of the main portal to the mine, two million gallons of acidic, metal-laden water came gushing out, turning the water of the Western orange for many miles, including the segment adjacent to Penny's ranch.

For two weeks, media attention was focused on the region. The river, a popular destination for rafters, kayakers, and fishing, was closed to all recreation. EPA and state officials ordered municipal water suppliers, residential well owners, farmers, and ranchers to shut off their irrigation systems and taps while investigation and testing ensued. They also advised ranchers to keep their livestock out of the river.

According to the state health department, water samples taken immediately after the spill from the Western River near Penny's house contained high concentrations of a number of heavy metals, including cadmium, chromium, copper, beryllium, barium, lead, nickel, and zinc. Mercury and arsenic were also present in elevated concentrations. After two weeks had passed, the water returned to its normal color, a permanent plug was placed at the mine, and the advisories were lifted.

A couple months later, in September, testing by the EPA revealed persistent elevated metal levels in the riverbed. Of particular concern were chromium and lead. Chromium was measured at 4.7 parts per million (ppm) in sediments in the bed of the river. In baseline "clean" sediments in a nearby (but unconnected) water body, chromium was measured at 1.0 ppm. The EPA's maximum safe level for chromium in drinking water under the Safe Drinking Water Act is 0.01 ppm. EPA measured lead concentrations in Western River sediments at 9.9 ppm. Baseline levels elsewhere in the region read at 2.0. The EPA says any lead contamination in drinking water is unsafe. Beryllium and nickel, which have been linked to cancer and other health problems in studies involving laboratory animals, remain elevated in the water column as well. Many of these contaminants occur naturally in rocks, soils, and plants, but industrial activities can result in much higher concentrations in water and soil than would otherwise be found naturally.

Penny uses water from an underground well on her property to meet her domestic and stock-watering needs. When she heard about the EPA's test results, she got scared. She immediately boiled a glass jar to sterilize it and filled it with well water from her tap. She sent her water sample to M&M Labs for testing. The lab report showed that her water had normal (safe) levels of bacteria, but unusually high levels of arsenic, chromium, lead, and nickel. Penny had never had her well water tested for anything but bacteria, and she had to pay extra—$500—to have more sophisticated tests done. She thought the test would give her some peace of mind, but it has done just the opposite. For now, she is drinking bottled water, but her cattle continue to drink from stock tanks filled with well water. Prior to the spill, she had also allowed them to drink from the Western River while they grazed in an adjacent meadow, but she has kept her cattle from that parcel since the spill.

Penny is also concerned about the stigma of contamination on the value of her ranch, which she inherited from her father in 2010. At the time, its appraised value, including legal rights to the groundwater, was $11,100,000. Penny's sister-in-law Rhonda, a local realtor, says that ranch values in the Gunsmoke area have decreased dramatically since the spill, in some cases as much as 30%, but Penny has not yet sought a new appraisal for her ranch.

Official investigations into the spill continue, but the press has had a field day with the event. When Penny retained your services, she showed you the following newspaper clipping, published just a few days after the spill.

GUNSMOKE DAILY PRESS

Town Struggles With Spill

By Walton White
July 31, 20XX

GUNSMOKE, NM. The town of Gunsmoke continues to struggle in the aftermath of the Gold Summit spill. Residents and tourists alike are being advised to stay away from the Western River and to utilize alternative water supplies. Company officials refused to comment, but Homer Samson, Summit's backhoe operator who worked on the mine closure, lamented, "I am so sorry and so sad for the town of Gunsmoke. My family has lived in Gunsmoke for over a decade, and I've always been proud of my work because I know how important the mining industry is to the region." Samson remarked, "I was under a great deal of pressure to finish the Gold Summit job quickly, with only myself and an inexperienced skeleton crew of two other temporary employees, in order to keep the costs down, since Summit no longer makes any money off that old mine."

Samson, who had assisted with mine closures when a few other regional gold and silver mines were shut down recently due to falling prices for precious metals, explained that, in his experience, the Gold Summit closure was unusual, in that other companies had employed at least a dozen workers trained to use heavy equipment and at least one or more consultants with expertise in surface and groundwater hydrology, geology, and contaminant transport. According to Samson, "An accident like this should never happen." He and other workers at the adjacent Galactic Mine used a drill to bore into the mine and check the level of wastewater in it prior to excavating backfill at the portal. Samson said, "Drilling takes time and money, but it's worth it; there were no problems at Galactic."

According to Eileen Ernest, a remediation specialist at the U.S. EPA, there are thousands of defunct and abandoned mines across New Mexico and other western states. The conditions that led to the Gold Summit disaster, says Ernest, "are by no means isolated, but instead are surprisingly prevalent." For now, government officials and residents of Gunsmoke and the surrounding area have their hands full with the Gold Summit spill.

 ## Points to Consider

Penny wants you to look into her options for obtaining compensation from Summit Corp. At this point, Penny is concerned only with compensation, and intends to leave any type of cleanup requirements to government authorities.

Task One. For purposes of this question, assume that the Gold Summit spill involved a prohibited discharge of a pollutant from a point source under the Clean Water Act (CWA). Can Penny use the CWA's citizen suit provision to obtain compensation for monetary damages? Does the CWA preempt or displace other types of statutory or common law claims she might bring? *See* Chapter 4 (Clean Water Act); 33 U.S.C. §§ 1365(a)(1), (e), 1370 (provided below).

Task Two. Are there any other federal environmental laws that might be useful to Penny's cause? If so, can Penny pursue both a statutory citizen suit or recovery action and a common law tort action, or do federal environmental statutes preempt or displace common law lawsuits? *See* Chapter 5 (Comprehensive Environmental Response, Compensation, and Liability Act); Chapter 6 (Resource Conservation and Recovery Act); 42 U.S.C. **§§** 6972(f), 9614, 9652, 9659 (provided below).

Task Three. You have decided to bring common law tort claims against Summit Corp. on Penny's behalf. Based on the facts as you know them, what claims should you pursue? In addition to property damages, can Penny receive payment for the possibility of contracting diseases or cancer in the future and/or the cost of future medical and veterinary bills for monitoring her health and the condition of her cattle? Write an outline that you could use to advise Penny about the merits of her potential tort claims and damage remedies.

Task Four. What information will you need to develop and pursue tort claims on Penny's behalf? In particular, what will you need to do to find out whether the contaminants in the river and in Penny's well came from the Gold Summit spill? Consider the following points:

1. Can you obtain all of the information you'll need through a Freedom of Information Act (FOIA) request to the U.S. EPA and/or other federal agencies with involvement in mining or pollution control? What information might you obtain from the state of New Mexico, using a state law FOIA equivalent? Draft a list of the kinds of information you would request, taking note of any potential exemptions provided in FOIA. If appropriate, you might request a fee waiver or a reduced charge for the production of relevant records. Online "Frequently Asked Questions" and forms may help you think through your request. For the federal agencies, see U.S. Dep't of Justice, FOIA.gov,

http://www.foia.gov/how-to.html. For New Mexico, see National Freedom of Information Coalition, http://www.nfoic.org/ new-mexico-sample-foia-request.

2. Assuming that you'll need to engage in discovery, draft a discovery plan. Refer to Federal Rules of Civil Procedure 26-34 (relevant provisions can be found in Appendix B). Be sure to address the following issues:

a) Will you need to make a Request for Entry or Inspection of Land under Fed. R. Civ. P. Rule 34 and, if so, what will you include in this request? (To help you think this through, fill out the form provided at the end of this chapter.) On a related note, will the test results of Penny's groundwater from M&M Labs be sufficient to establish contamination, or will additional testing of the well water, the river water, or the surrounding soils be necessary? How will you obtain the necessary samples and tests?

b) What documents will you request under Fed. R. Civ. P. Rule 34, and from whom?

c) Fed. R. Civ. P. Rule 26(a)(1) will require you to make initial disclosures to opposing counsel, typically within 60 to 90 days after the complaint has been filed (within 14 days after the parties conduct a Rule 26(f) conference to discuss a discovery plan and other matters). Given this tight time-line, you should be ready to conduct a factual background investigation to identify individuals who would likely have discoverable information. Accordingly, draft a list of individuals that you may call upon to support your claims.

d) Who will you need to depose? What questions will you ask? Can you avoid engaging in depositions and instead simply interview Mr. Samson or other potentially knowledgeable individuals? *See* Model Rules of Professional Conduct 1.13 (organizations); 4.2 (ex parte communications); and 4.3 (unrepresented persons). Would your response regarding Mr. Samson vary if Samson had been laid off by Summit Corp.?

e) What type of experts might you need to employ, and how will you identify reputable experts? In light of Fed. R. Civ. P. Rules 26(a)(2) and 30, should you retain them as consulting experts or should you treat them as expert witnesses?

f) If you think you'll need experts to testify in court to support your claims, how will you ensure that they meet Fed. Rule of Evidence 702 (provided below)? Consider the *Daubert* test, which, as you may recall from Civil Procedure or Evidence, requires trial court judges to act as gatekeepers to exclude unreliable or irrelevant expert testimony. *Daubert v. Merrell Dow Pharmaceuticals, Inc.*, 509 U.S. 579 (1993).

> Clean Water Act

CWA § 505, 33 U.S.C. § 1365. Citizen suits

(a) [A]ny citizen may commence a civil action on his own behalf—

(1) against any person (including (i) the United States, and (ii) any other governmental instrumentality or agency to the extent permitted by the eleventh amendment to the Constitution) who is alleged to be in violation of (A) an effluent standard or limitation under this chapter or (B) an order issued by the Administrator or a State with respect to such a standard or limitation. . . .

The district courts shall have jurisdiction . . . to enforce such an effluent standard or limitation, or such an order, . . . and to apply any appropriate civil penalties under section 1319(d) of this title.

* * *

(e) Nothing in this section shall restrict any right which any person (or class of persons) may have under any statute or common law to seek enforcement of any effluent standard or limitation or to seek any other relief (including relief against the Administrator or a State agency).

CWA § 510, 33 U.S.C. § 1370. State authority

Except as expressly provided in this chapter, nothing in this chapter shall (1) preclude or deny the right of any State or political subdivision thereof or interstate agency to adopt or enforce (A) any standard or limitation respecting discharges of pollutants, or (B) any requirement respecting control or abatement of pollution; except that if an effluent limitation, or other limitation, effluent standard, prohibition, pretreatment standard, or standard of performance is in effect under this chapter, such State or political subdivision or interstate agency may not adopt or enforce any effluent limitation, or other limitation, effluent standard, prohibition, pretreatment standard, or standard of performance which is less stringent than the effluent limitation, or other limitation, effluent standard, prohibition, pretreatment standard, or standard of performance under this chapter . . . .

> Resource Conservation and Recovery Act

RCRA, 42 U.S.C. § 6972. Citizen Suits

* * *

(a)(1) [A]ny person may commence a civil action on his own behalf . . .

(B) against any person, . . . including any past or present generator, past or present transporter, or past or present owner or operator of a treatment, storage, or disposal facility, who has contributed or who is contributing to the past or present handling, storage, treatment, transportation, or disposal of any solid or hazardous waste which may present an imminent and substantial endangerment to health or the environment . . .

The district court shall have jurisdiction, without regard to the amount in controversy or the citizenship of the parties, . . . to restrain any person who has contributed or who is contributing to the past or present handling, storage, treatment, transportation, or disposal of any solid or hazardous waste referred to in paragraph (1)(B), to order such person to take such other action as may be necessary, or both, . . . and to apply any appropriate civil penalties under section 6928(a) and (g) of this title.

(f) Nothing in this section shall restrict any right which any person (or class of persons) may have under any statute or common law to seek enforcement of any standard or requirement relating to the management of solid waste or hazardous waste, or to seek any other relief (including relief against the Administrator or a State agency).

* * *

> CERCLA

CERCLA § 114, 42 U.S.C. § 9614. Relationship to other law

(a) Nothing in this chapter shall be construed or interpreted as preempting any State from imposing any additional liability or requirements with respect to the release of hazardous substances within such State.

* * *

CERCLA § 302, 42 U.S.C. § 9652. Effective dates; savings provisions

* * *

(d) Nothing in this chapter shall affect or modify in any way the obligations or liabilities of any person under other Federal or State law, including common law, with respect to releases of hazardous substances or other pollutants or contaminants. The provisions of this chapter shall not be considered, interpreted, or construed in any way as reflecting a determination, in part or whole, of policy regarding the inapplicability of strict liability, or strict liability doctrines, to activities relating to hazardous substances, pollutants, or contaminants or other such activities.

CERCLA § 310, 42 U.S.C. § 9659. Citizen Suits

(a) Except as provided in subsections (d) and (e) of this section and in section 9613(h) of this title (relating to timing of judicial review), any person may commence a civil action on his own behalf—

> (1) against any person . . . who is alleged to be in violation of any standard, regulation, condition, requirement, or order which has become effective pursuant to this chapter. . . .

(c) The district court shall have jurisdiction in actions brought under subsection (a)(1) of this section to enforce the standard, regulation, condition, requirement, or order concerned . . . , to order such action as may be necessary to correct the violation, and to impose any civil penalty provided for the violation. . . .

(h) This chapter does not affect or otherwise impair the rights of any person under Federal, State, or common law, except with respect to the timing of review as provided in section 9613(h) of this title or as otherwise provided in section 9658 of this title (relating to actions under State law).

* * *

> **Federal Rules of Evidence**

Federal Rules of Evidence Rule 702. Testimony by Expert Witnesses

A witness who is qualified as an expert by knowledge, skill, experience, training, or education may testify in the form of an opinion or otherwise if:

(a) the expert's scientific, technical, or other specialized knowledge will help the trier of fact to understand the evidence or to determine a fact in issue;

(b) the testimony is based on sufficient facts or data;

(c) the testimony is the product of reliable principles and methods; and

(d) the expert has reliably applied the principles and methods to the facts of the case.

* * *

IN THE _____ COURT
FOR THE DISTRICT OF _____

Penny Peterson,⠀⠀⠀⠀⠀)
⠀⠀⠀Plaintiff⠀⠀⠀⠀⠀⠀)
⠀⠀⠀⠀⠀⠀⠀⠀⠀⠀⠀⠀)
v.⠀⠀⠀⠀⠀⠀⠀⠀⠀⠀⠀)⠀⠀Civil Action No.:
⠀⠀⠀⠀⠀⠀⠀⠀⠀⠀⠀⠀)
Summit Corp.,⠀⠀⠀⠀⠀)
⠀⠀⠀Defendant⠀⠀⠀⠀⠀)

PLAINTIFF'S RULE 34 REQUEST TO PERMIT ENTRY UPON LAND OR OTHER PROPERTY FOR INSPECTION AND OTHER PURPOSES

Pursuant to Rule 34 of the Federal Rules of Civil Procedure, the plaintiff in the above captioned case requests the defendant to permit the plaintiff, or an agent of the plaintiff, to enter upon the following land and property for the purposes of inspection, measuring, surveying, photographing, testing or sampling:

⠀⠀⠀· [Describe the property to be entered and inspected]

The plaintiff or plaintiff's agent will also inspect, measure, survey, photograph, test or sample the following objects or operations on the same land and property:

⠀⠀⠀· [Describe the objects and operations to be inspected]

The plaintiff requests that such entry and inspection take place on the date _____ , unless the defendant designates another date agreed to by the plaintiff.

The plaintiff requests that the defendant respond to this request within 30 days after the service of this request.

[(s)] _____
Attorney for Plaintiff

Address: _____

_____

_____

Appendix A
Model Rules of Professional Conduct[1]

▶ Rule 1.1 Competence

A lawyer shall provide competent representation to a client. Competent representation requires the legal knowledge, skill, thoroughness and preparation reasonably necessary for the representation.

▶ Rule 1.1 Competence – Comment

[1] In determining whether a lawyer employs the requisite knowledge and skill in a particular matter, relevant factors include the relative complexity and specialized nature of the matter, the lawyer's general experience, the lawyer's training and experience in the field in question, the preparation and study the lawyer is able to give the matter and whether it is feasible to refer the matter to, or associate or consult with, a lawyer of established competence in the field in question. In many instances, the required proficiency is that of a general practitioner. Expertise in a particular field of law may be required in some circumstances.

[2] A lawyer need not necessarily have special training or prior experience to handle legal problems of a type with which the lawyer is unfamiliar. A newly admitted lawyer can be as competent as a practitioner with long experience. Some important legal skills, such as the analysis of precedent, the evaluation of evidence and legal drafting, are required in all legal problems. Perhaps the most fundamental legal skill consists of determining what kind of legal problems a situation may involve, a skill that necessarily transcends any particular specialized knowledge. A lawyer can provide adequate representation in a wholly novel field through necessary study. Competent representation

1   Model Rules of Professional Conduct @2016 the American Bar Association

can also be provided through the association of a lawyer of established competence in the field in question.

▶ Rule 1.2 Scope of Representation and Allocation of Authority Between Client and Lawyer

(a) Subject to paragraph[ ] . . . (d), a lawyer shall abide by a client's decisions concerning the objectives of representation and, as required by Rule 1.4, shall consult with the client as to the means by which they are to be pursued. A lawyer may take such action on behalf of the client as is impliedly authorized to carry out the representation.

(b) A lawyer's representation of a client, including representation by appointment, does not constitute an endorsement of the client's political, economic, social or moral views or activities. . . .

(d) A lawyer shall not counsel a client to engage, or assist a client, in conduct that the lawyer knows is criminal or fraudulent, but a lawyer may discuss the legal consequences of any proposed course of conduct with a client and may counsel or assist a client to make a good faith effort to determine the validity, scope, meaning or application of the law.

* * *

▶ Rule 1.3 Diligence

A lawyer shall act with reasonable diligence and promptness in representing a client.

▶ Rule 1.3 Diligence—Comment

[1] A lawyer should pursue a matter on behalf of a client despite opposition, obstruction or personal inconvenience to the lawyer, and

take whatever lawful and ethical measures are required to vindicate a client's cause or endeavor. A lawyer must also act with commitment and dedication to the interests of the client and with zeal in advocacy upon the client's behalf. A lawyer is not bound, however, to press for every advantage that might be realized for a client. For example, a lawyer may have authority to exercise professional discretion in determining the means by which a matter should be pursued. . . . The lawyer's duty to act with reasonable diligence does not require the use of offensive tactics or preclude the treating of all persons involved in the legal process with courtesy and respect. . . .

▶ Rule 1.4 Communication

(a) A lawyer shall: . . .

(2) reasonably consult with the client about the means by which the client's objectives are to be accomplished;

(3) keep the client reasonably informed about the status of the matter; . . .

(5) consult with the client about any relevant limitation on the lawyer's conduct when the lawyer knows that the client expects assistance not permitted by the Rules of Professional Conduct or other law.

(b) A lawyer shall explain a matter to the extent reasonably necessary to permit the client to make informed decisions regarding the representation.

▶ Rule 1.6 Confidentiality of Information

(a) A lawyer shall not reveal information relating to the representation of a client unless the client gives informed consent, the disclosure is impliedly authorized in order to carry out the representation or the disclosure is permitted by paragraph (b).

(b) A lawyer may reveal information relating to the representation of a client to the extent the lawyer reasonably believes necessary:

> (1) to prevent reasonably certain death or substantial bodily harm;

> (2) to prevent the client from committing a crime or fraud that is reasonably certain to result in substantial injury to the financial interests or property of another and in furtherance of which the client has used or is using the lawyer's services;

> (3) to prevent, mitigate or rectify substantial injury to the financial interests or property of another that is reasonably certain to result or has resulted from the client's commission of a crime or fraud in furtherance of which the client has used the lawyer's services . . . .

▶ Rule 1.7 Conflict of Interest: Current Clients

(a) Except as provided in paragraph (b), a lawyer shall not represent a client if the representation involves a concurrent conflict of interest. A concurrent conflict of interest exists if:

the representation of one client will be directly adverse to another client; or

> (2) there is a significant risk that the representation of one or more clients will be materially limited by the lawyer's responsibilities to another client, a former client or a third person or by a personal interest of the lawyer.

(b) Notwithstanding the existence of a concurrent conflict of interest under paragraph (a), a lawyer may represent a client if:

(1) the lawyer reasonably believes that the lawyer will be able to provide competent and diligent representation to each affected client;

the representation is not prohibited by law;

(3) the representation does not involve the assertion of a claim by
one client against another client represented by the lawyer in the
same litigation or other proceeding before a tribunal; and

(4) each affected client gives informed consent, confirmed in
writing.

▶ Rule 1.11 Special Conflicts of Interest For Former and Current Government Officers and Employees

(a) Except as law may otherwise expressly permit, a lawyer who has
formerly served as a public officer or employee of the government:

* * *

(2) shall not otherwise represent a client in connection with a matter in which the lawyer participated personally and substantially
as a public officer or employee, unless the appropriate government
agency gives its informed consent, confirmed in writing, to the
representation.

* * *

(c) Except as law may otherwise expressly permit, a lawyer having
information that the lawyer knows is confidential government information about a person acquired when the lawyer was a public officer
or employee, may not represent a private client whose interests are
adverse to that person in a matter in which the information could be
used to the material disadvantage of that person. As used in this Rule,

the term "confidential government information" means information that has been obtained under governmental authority and which, at the time this Rule is applied, the government is prohibited by law from disclosing to the public or has a legal privilege not to disclose and which is not otherwise available to the public. A firm with which that lawyer is associated may undertake or continue representation in the matter only if the disqualified lawyer is timely screened from any participation in the matter and is apportioned no part of the fee therefrom.

(d) Except as law may otherwise expressly permit, a lawyer currently serving as a public officer or employee: . . . (2) shall not: (i) participate in a matter in which the lawyer participated personally and substantially while in private practice or nongovernmental employment, unless the appropriate government agency gives its informed consent, confirmed in writing. . . .

(e) As used in this Rule, the term "matter" includes:

(1) any judicial or other proceeding, application, request for a ruling or other determination, contract, claim, controversy, investigation, charge, accusation, arrest or other particular matter involving a specific party or parties, and

(2) any other matter covered by the conflict of interest rules of the appropriate government agency.

▶ Rule 1.13 Organization as Client

(a) A lawyer employed or retained by an organization represents the organization acting through its duly authorized constituents.

(b) If a lawyer for an organization knows that an officer, employee or other person associated with the organization is engaged in action, intends to act or refuses to act in a matter related to the representation that is a violation of a legal obligation to the organization, or a violation of law that reasonably might be imputed to the organization, and that is likely to result in substantial injury to the organization, then the lawyer shall proceed as is reasonably necessary in the best interest of the organization. Unless the lawyer reasonably believes that it is not necessary in the best interest of the organization to do so, the lawyer shall refer the matter to higher authority in the organization, including, if warranted by the circumstances to the highest authority that can act on behalf of the organization as determined by applicable law.

(c) Except as provided in paragraph (d), if

(1) despite the lawyer's efforts in accordance with paragraph (b) the highest authority that can act on behalf of the organization insists upon or fails to address in a timely and appropriate manner an action, or a refusal to act, that is clearly a violation of law, and

(2) the lawyer reasonably believes that the violation is reasonably certain to result in substantial injury to the organization,

then the lawyer may reveal information relating to the representation whether or not Rule 1.6 permits such disclosure, but only if and to the extent the lawyer reasonably believes necessary to prevent substantial injury to the organization.

(d) Paragraph (c) shall not apply with respect to information relating to a lawyer's representation of an organization to investigate an alleged violation of law, or to defend the organization or an officer, employee or other constituent associated with the organization against a claim arising out of an alleged violation of law.

* * *

(f) In dealing with an organization's directors, officers, employees, members, shareholders or other constituents, a lawyer shall explain the identity of the client when the lawyer knows or reasonably should know that the organization's interests are adverse to those of the constituents with whom the lawyer is dealing.

* * *

▶ Rule 1.16 Declining or Terminating Representation

(a) Except as stated in paragraph (c), a lawyer shall not represent a client or, where representation has commenced, shall withdraw from the representation of a client if:

(1) the representation will result in violation of the rules of professional conduct or other law;

(2) the lawyer's physical or mental condition materially impairs the lawyer's ability to represent the client; or

(3) the lawyer is discharged.

(b) Except as stated in paragraph (c), a lawyer may withdraw from representing a client if:

(1) withdrawal can be accomplished without material adverse effect on the interests of the client;

(2) the client persists in a course of action involving the lawyer's services that the lawyer reasonably believes is criminal or fraudulent;

(3) the client has used the lawyer's services to perpetrate a crime or fraud;

(4) the client insists upon taking action that the lawyer considers re-
pugnant or with which the lawyer has a fundamental disagreement;

(5) the client fails substantially to fulfill an obligation to the lawyer
regarding the lawyer's services and has been given reasonable
warning that the lawyer will withdraw unless the obligation is
fulfilled;

(6) the representation will result in an unreasonable financial
burden on the lawyer or has been rendered unreasonably difficult
by the client; or

(7) other good cause for withdrawal exists.

* * *

(d) Upon termination of representation, a lawyer shall take steps to
the extent reasonably practicable to protect a client's interests, such as
giving reasonable notice to the client, allowing time for employment
of other counsel, surrendering papers and property to which the client
is entitled and refunding any advance payment of fee or expense that
has not been earned or incurred. . . .

* * *

▶ Rule 2.1 Advisor

In representing a client, a lawyer shall exercise independent professional judgment and render candid advice. In rendering advice, a
lawyer may refer not only to law but to other considerations such as
moral, economic, social and political factors, that may be relevant to
the client's situation.

▶ Rule 3.1 Meritorious Claims and Contentions

A lawyer shall not bring or defend a proceeding, or assert or controvert an issue therein, unless there is a basis in law and fact for doing so that is not frivolous, which includes a good faith argument for an extension, modification or reversal of existing law. A lawyer for the defendant in a criminal proceeding, or the respondent in a proceeding that could result in incarceration, may nevertheless so defend the proceeding as to require that every element of the case be established.

▶ Rule 3.1 Meritorious Claims and Contentions—Comment

[1] The advocate has a duty to use legal procedure for the fullest benefit of the client's cause, but also a duty not to abuse legal procedure. The law, both procedural and substantive, establishes the limits within which an advocate may proceed. However, the law is not always clear and never is static. Accordingly, in determining the proper scope of advocacy, account must be taken of the law's ambiguities and potential for change.

[2] The filing of an action or defense or similar action taken for a client is not frivolous merely because the facts have not first been fully substantiated or because the lawyer expects to develop vital evidence only by discovery. What is required of lawyers, however, is that they inform themselves about the facts of their clients' cases and the applicable law and determine that they can make good faith arguments in support of their clients' positions. Such action is not frivolous even though the lawyer believes that the client's position ultimately will not prevail. The action is frivolous, however, if the lawyer is unable either to make a good faith argument on the merits of the action taken or to support the action taken by a good faith argument for an extension, modification or reversal of existing law.

* * *

▶ Rule 3.3 Candor Toward the Tribunal

(a) A lawyer shall not knowingly:

(1) make a false statement of fact or law to a tribunal[2] or fail to correct a false statement of material fact or law previously made to the tribunal by the lawyer;

(2) fail to disclose to the tribunal legal authority in the controlling jurisdiction known to the lawyer to be directly adverse to the position of the client and not disclosed by opposing counsel; or

(3) offer evidence that the lawyer knows to be false. If a lawyer, the lawyer's client, or a witness called by the lawyer, has offered material evidence and the lawyer comes to know of its falsity, the lawyer shall take reasonable remedial measures, including, if necessary, disclosure to the tribunal. A lawyer may refuse to offer evidence, other than the testimony of a defendant in a criminal matter, that the lawyer reasonably believes is false. . . .

---

2   Rule 1.0(m) of the Model Rules defines a "tribunal" as follows:

"Tribunal" denotes a court, an arbitrator in a binding arbitration proceeding or a legislative body, administrative agency or other body acting in an adjudicative capacity. A legislative body, administrative agency or other body acts in an adjudicative capacity when a neutral official, after the presentation of evidence or legal argument by a party or parties, will render a binding legal judgment directly affecting a party's interests in a particular matter.

▶ Rule 3.7 Lawyer as Witness

(a) A lawyer shall not act as advocate at a trial in which the lawyer is likely to be a necessary witness unless:

(1) the testimony relates to an uncontested issue;

(2) the testimony relates to the nature and value of legal services rendered in the case; or

(3) disqualification of the lawyer would work substantial hardship on the client.

* * *

▶ Rule 3.8 Special Responsibilities of a Prosecutor

The prosecutor in a criminal case shall:

(a) refrain from prosecuting a charge that the prosecutor knows is not supported by probable cause; . . .

(d) make timely disclosure to the defense of all evidence or information known to the prosecutor that tends to negate the guilt of the accused or mitigates the offense, and, in connection with sentencing, disclose to the defense and to the tribunal all unprivileged mitigating information known to the prosecutor, except when the prosecutor is relieved of this responsibility by a protective order of the tribunal; . . .

(f) except for statements that are necessary to inform the public of the nature and extent of the prosecutor's action and that serve a legitimate law enforcement purpose, refrain from making extrajudicial comments that have a substantial likelihood of heightening public condemnation of the accused and exercise reasonable care to prevent investigators, law enforcement personnel, employees or other persons assisting or associated with the prosecutor in a criminal case from making an extrajudicial statement that the prosecutor would be prohibited from making under Rule 3.6 [regarding Trial Publicity] or this Rule. . . .

▶ Rule 4.1 Truthfulness in Statements to Others

In the course of representing a client a lawyer shall not knowingly:

(a) make a false statement of material fact or law to a third person; or

(b) fail to disclose a material fact to a third person when disclosure is necessary to avoid assisting a criminal or fraudulent act by a client, unless disclosure is prohibited by Rule 1.6.

▶ Rule 4.2 Communication with Person Represented by Counsel

In representing a client, a lawyer shall not communicate about the subject of the representation with a person the lawyer knows to be represented by another lawyer in the matter, unless the lawyer has the consent of the other lawyer or is authorized to do so by law or a court order.

▶ Rule 4.3 Dealing with Unrepresented Person

In dealing on behalf of a client with a person who is not represented by counsel, a lawyer shall not state or imply that the lawyer is disinterested. When the lawyer knows or reasonably should know that the unrepresented person misunderstands the lawyer's role in the matter, the lawyer shall make reasonable efforts to correct the misunderstanding. The lawyer shall not give legal advice to an unrepresented person, other than the advice to secure counsel, if the lawyer knows or reasonably should know that the interests of such a person are or have a reasonable possibility of being in conflict with the interests of the client.

▶ Rule 6.1 Voluntary Pro Bono Publico Service

Every lawyer has a professional responsibility to provide legal services to those unable to pay. A lawyer should aspire to render at least (50) hours of pro bono publico legal services per year. In fulfilling this responsibility, the lawyer should:

(a) provide a substantial majority of the (50) hours of legal services without fee or expectation of fee to:

(1) persons of limited means or

(2) charitable, religious, civic, community, governmental and educational organizations in matters that are designed primarily to address the needs of persons of limited means; and

(b) provide any additional services through:

(1) delivery of legal services at no fee or substantially reduced fee to individuals, groups or organizations seeking to secure or protect civil rights, civil liberties or public rights, or charitable, religious, civic, community, governmental and educational organizations in matters in furtherance of their organizational purposes, where the payment of standard legal fees would significantly deplete the organization's economic resources or would be otherwise inappropriate;

(2) delivery of legal services at a substantially reduced fee to persons of limited means; or

(3) participation in activities for improving the law, the legal system or the legal profession. . . .

Appendix B
Federal Rules of Civil Procedure, Administrative Procedure Act, and Freedom of Information Act

Federal Rules of Civil Procedure

▶ **Rule 11. Signing Pleadings, Motions, and Other Papers; Representations to the Court; Sanctions**

* * *

(b) Representations to the Court.

By presenting to the court a pleading, written motion, or other paper—whether by signing, filing, submitting, or later advocating it—an attorney or unrepresented party certifies that to the best of the person's knowledge, information, and belief, formed after an inquiry reasonable under the circumstances:

   (1) it is not being presented for any improper purpose, such as to harass, cause unnecessary delay, or needlessly increase the cost of litigation;

   (2) the claims, defenses, and other legal contentions are warranted by existing law or by a nonfrivolous argument for extending, modifying, or reversing existing law or for establishing new law;

   (3) the factual contentions have evidentiary support or, if specifically so identified, will likely have evidentiary support after a reasonable opportunity for further investigation or discovery; and

(4) the denials of factual contentions are warranted on the evidence or, if specifically so identified, are reasonably based on belief or a lack of information.

(c) Sanctions.

(1) In General. If, after notice and a reasonable opportunity to respond, the court determines that Rule 11(b) has been violated, the court may impose an appropriate sanction on any attorney, law firm, or party that violated the rule or is responsible for the violation. Absent exceptional circumstances, a law firm must be held jointly responsible for a violation committed by its partner, associate, or employee. . .

* * *

(4) Nature of a Sanction. A sanction imposed under this rule must be limited to what suffices to deter repetition of the conduct or comparable conduct by others similarly situated. The sanction may include nonmonetary directives; an order to pay a penalty into court; or, if imposed on motion and warranted for effective deterrence, an order directing payment to the movant of part or all of the reasonable attorney's fees and other expenses directly resulting from the violation.

▶ **Rule 12. Defenses and Objections: When and How Presented; Motion for Judgment on the Pleadings; Consolidating Motions; Waiving Defenses; Pretrial Hearing**

(a) Time to Serve a Responsive Pleading.

(1) Unless another time is specified by this rule or a federal statute, the time for serving a responsive pleading is as follows:

(A) A defendant must serve an answer:

 (i) within 21 days after being served with the summons and complaint; or

 (ii) if it has timely waived service under Rule 4(d), within 60 days after the request for a waiver was sent, or within 90 days after it was sent to the defendant outside any judicial district of the United States.

(B) A party must serve an answer to a counterclaim or cross-claim within 21 days after being served with the pleading that states the counterclaim or crossclaim.

(C) A party must serve a reply to an answer within 21 days after being served with an order to reply, unless the order specifies a different time.

(2) The United States, a United States agency, or a United States officer or employee sued only in an official capacity must serve an answer to a complaint, counterclaim, or crossclaim within 60 days after service on the United States attorney. . . .

(b) How to Present Defenses. Every defense to a claim for relief in any pleading must be asserted in the responsive pleading if one is required. But a party may assert the following defenses by motion:

(1) lack of subject-matter jurisdiction;

(2) lack of personal jurisdiction;

(3) improper venue;

(4) insufficient process;

(5) insufficient service of process;

(6) failure to state a claim upon which relief can be granted; and

(7) failure to join a party under Rule 19.

A motion asserting any of these defenses must be made before pleading if a responsive pleading is allowed. If a pleading sets out a claim for relief that does not require a responsive pleading, an opposing party may assert at trial any defense to that claim. No defense or objection is waived by joining it with one or more other defenses or objections in a responsive pleading or in a motion.

(c) Motion for Judgment on the Pleadings. After the pleadings are closed—but early enough not to delay trial—a party may move for judgment on the pleadings.

(d) Result of Presenting Matters Outside the Pleadings. If, on a motion under Rule 12(b)(6) or 12(c), matters outside the pleadings are presented to and not excluded by the court, the motion must be treated as one for summary judgment under Rule 56. All parties must be given a reasonable opportunity to present all the material that is pertinent to the motion.

* * *

(h) Waiving and Preserving Certain Defenses.

(1) When Some Are Waived. A party waives any defense listed in Rule 12(b)(2)–(5) by:

(A) omitting it from a motion in the circumstances described in Rule 12(g)(2); or

(B) failing to either:

(i) make it by motion under this rule; or

(ii) include it in a responsive pleading or in an amendment allowed by Rule 15(a)(1) as a matter of course.

(2) When to Raise Others. Failure to state a claim upon which relief can be granted, to join a person required by Rule 19(b), or to state a legal defense to a claim may be raised:

(A) in any pleading allowed or ordered under Rule 7(a);

(B) by a motion under Rule 12(c); or

(C) at trial.

(3) Lack of Subject-Matter Jurisdiction. If the court determines at any time that it lacks subject-matter jurisdiction, the court must dismiss the action.

* * *

▶ Rule 26. Duty to Disclose; General Provisions Governing Discovery

(a) Required Disclosures.

(1) Initial Disclosure.

(A) Except as exempted by Rule 26(a)(1)(B) or as otherwise stipulated or ordered by the court, a party must, without awaiting a discovery request, provide to the other parties:

(i) the name and, if known, the address and telephone number of each individual likely to have discoverable information—along with the subjects of that information—that the disclosing party may use to support its claims or defenses, unless the use would be solely for impeachment;

(ii) a copy—or a description by category and location—of all documents, electronically stored information, and tangible things that the disclosing party has in its possession, custody, or control and may use to support its claims or defenses, unless the use would be solely for impeachment;

(iii) a computation of each category of damages claimed by the disclosing party—who must also make available for inspection and copying as under Rule 34 the documents or other evidentiary material, unless privileged or protected from disclosure, on which each computation is based, including materials bearing on the nature and extent of injuries suffered . . .

(B) The following proceedings are exempt from initial disclosure: . . . (i) an action for review on an administrative record;

* * *

(E) A party must make its initial disclosures based on the information then reasonably available to it. A party is not excused from making its disclosures because it has not fully investigated the case or because it challenges the sufficiency of another party's disclosures or because another party has not made its disclosures.

(2) Disclosure of Expert Testimony.

(A) In addition to the disclosures required by Rule 26(a)(1), a party must disclose to the other parties the identity of any witness it may use at trial to present evidence under Federal Rule of Evidence 702, 703, or 705.

(B) Witnesses Who Must Provide a Written Report. Unless otherwise stipulated or ordered by the court, this disclosure must be accompanied by a written report—prepared and signed by the witness—if the witness is one retained or specially employed to provide expert testimony in the case or one whose duties as the party's employee regularly involve giving expert testimony. The report must contain:

(i) a complete statement of all opinions the witness will express and the basis and reasons for them;

(ii) the facts or data considered by the witness in forming them;

(iii) any exhibits that will be used to summarize or support them;

(iv) the witness's qualifications, including a list of all publications authored in the previous 10 years;

(v) a list of all other cases in which, during the previous 4 years, the witness testified as an expert at trial or by deposition; and

(vi) a statement of the compensation to be paid for the study and testimony in the case.

(C) Witnesses Who Do Not Provide a Written Report. Unless otherwise stipulated or ordered by the court, if the witness is not required to provide a written report, this disclosure must state:

(i) the subject matter on which the witness is expected to present evidence under Federal Rule of Evidence 702 . . . ; and

(ii) a summary of the facts and opinions to which the witness is expected to testify. . . .

(b) Discovery Scope and Limits.

(1) Scope in General. Unless otherwise limited by court order, the scope of discovery is as follows: Parties may obtain discovery regarding any nonprivileged matter that is relevant to any party's claim or defense—including the existence, description, nature, custody, condition, and location of any documents or other tangible things and the identity and location of persons who know of any discoverable matter. For good cause, the court may order discovery of any matter relevant to the subject matter involved in the action. Relevant information need not be admissible at the trial if the discovery appears reasonably calculated to lead to the discovery of admissible evidence. All discovery is subject to the limitations imposed by Rule 26(b)(2)(C).

(2) Limitations on Frequency and Extent.

(A) When Permitted. By order, the court may alter the limits in these rules on the number of depositions and interrogatories or on the length of depositions under Rule 30. By order or local rule, the court may also limit the number of requests under Rule 36.

(B) Specific Limitations on Electronically Stored Information. A party need not provide discovery of electronically stored information from sources that the party identifies as not reasonably accessible because of undue burden or cost. On motion to compel discovery or for a protective order, the party from whom discovery is sought must show that the information is not reasonably accessible because of undue burden or cost. If that showing is made, the court may nonetheless order discovery from such sources if the requesting party shows good cause, considering the limitations of Rule 26(b)(2)(C). The court may specify conditions for the discovery.

(C) When Required. On motion or on its own, the court must limit the frequency or extent of discovery otherwise allowed by these rules or by local rule if it determines that:

(i) the discovery sought is unreasonably cumulative or duplicative, or can be obtained from some other source that is more convenient, less burdensome, or less expensive;

(ii) the party seeking discovery has had ample opportunity to obtain the information by discovery in the action; or

(iii) the burden or expense of the proposed discovery out-weighs its likely benefit, considering the needs of the case, the amount in controversy, the parties' resources, the impor-tance of the issues at stake in the action, and the importance of the discovery in resolving the issues.

* * *

(5) Claiming Privilege or Protecting Trial-Preparation Materials.

(A) When a party withholds information otherwise discoverable by claiming that the information is privileged or subject to protection as trial-preparation material, the party must:

(i) expressly make the claim; and

(ii) describe the nature of the documents, communications, or tangible things not produced or disclosed—and do so in a manner that, without revealing information itself privileged or protected, will enable other parties to assess the claim.

(B) If information produced in discovery is subject to a claim of privilege or of protection as trial-preparation material, the party making the claim may notify any party that received the information of the claim and the basis for it. After being notified, a party must promptly return, sequester, or destroy the specified information and any copies it has; must not use or disclose the information until the claim is resolved; must take reasonable steps to retrieve the information if the party disclosed it before being notified; and may promptly present the information to the court under seal for a determination of the claim. The producing party must preserve the information until the claim is resolved.

(c) Protective Orders.

(1) A party or any person from whom discovery is sought may move for a protective order in the court where the action is pending—or as an alternative on matters relating to a deposition, in the court for the district where the deposition will be taken. The motion must include a certification that the movant has in good faith conferred or attempted to confer with other affected parties in an effort to resolve the dispute without court action. The court may, for good cause, issue an order to protect a party or person from annoyance, embarrassment, oppression, or undue burden or expense, including one or more of the following:

(A) forbidding the disclosure or discovery;

(B) specifying terms, including time and place, for the disclosure or discovery;

(C) prescribing a discovery method other than the one selected by the party seeking discovery;

(D) forbidding inquiry into certain matters, or limiting the scope of disclosure or discovery to certain matters;

(E) designating the persons who may be present while the discovery is conducted;

(F) requiring that a deposition be sealed and opened only on court order;

(G) requiring that a trade secret or other confidential research, development, or commercial information not be revealed or be revealed only in a specified way; and

(H) requiring that the parties simultaneously file specified documents or information in sealed envelopes, to be opened as the court directs.

(2) If a motion for a protective order is wholly or partly denied, the court may, on just terms, order that any party or person provide or permit discovery.

* * *

(g) Signing Disclosures and Discovery Requests, Responses, and Objections.

(1) Every disclosure . . . and every discovery request, response, or objection must be signed by at least one attorney of record in the attorney's own name—or by the party personally, if unrepresented—and must state the signer's address, e-mail address, and telephone number. By signing, an attorney or party certifies that to the best

of the person's knowledge, information, and belief formed after a reasonable inquiry:

(A) with respect to a disclosure, it is complete and correct as of the time it is made; and

(B) with respect to a discovery request, response, or objection, it is:

(i) consistent with these rules and warranted by existing law or by a nonfrivolous argument for extending, modifying, or reversing existing law, or for establishing new law;

(ii) not interposed for any improper purpose, such as to harass, cause unnecessary delay, or needlessly increase the cost of litigation; and

(iii) neither unreasonable nor unduly burdensome or expensive, considering the needs of the case, prior discovery in the case, the amount in controversy, and the importance of the issues at stake in the action.

(2) Other parties have no duty to act on an unsigned disclosure, request, response, or objection until it is signed, and the court must strike it unless a signature is promptly supplied after the omission is called to the attorney's or party's attention.

(3) If a certification violates this rule without substantial justification, the court, on motion or on its own, must impose an appropriate sanction on the signer, the party on whose behalf the signer was acting, or both. The sanction may include an order to pay the reasonable expenses, including attorney's fees, caused by the violation.

▶ Rule 33. Interrogatories to Parties

(a) In General.

(1) Number. Unless otherwise stipulated or ordered by the court, a party may serve on any other party no more than 25 written interrogatories, including all discrete subparts. Leave to serve additional interrogatories may be granted to the extent consistent with Rule 26(b)(1) and (2).

(2) Scope. An interrogatory may relate to any matter that may be inquired into under Rule 26(b). An interrogatory is not objectionable merely because it asks for an opinion or contention that relates to fact or the application of law to fact, but the court may order that the interrogatory need not be answered until designated discovery is complete, or until a pretrial conference or some other time.

* * *

▶ Rule 34. Producing Documents, Electronically Stored Information, and Tangible Things, or Entering onto Land, for Inspection and Other Purposes

(a) In General. A party may serve on any other party a request within the scope of Rule 26(b):

(1) to produce and permit the requesting party or its representative to inspect, copy, test, or sample the following items in the responding party's possession, custody, or control:

(A) any designated documents or electronically stored information—including writings, drawings, graphs, charts, photographs, sound recordings, images, and other data or data compilations—stored in any medium from which information can be obtained either directly or, if necessary, after translation by the responding party into a reasonably usable form; or

(B) any designated tangible things; or

(2) to permit entry onto designated land or other property possessed or controlled by the responding party, so that the requesting party may inspect, measure, survey, photograph, test, or sample the property or any designated object or operation on it.

(b) Procedure.

(1) Contents of the Request. The request:

(A) must describe with reasonable particularity each item or category of items to be inspected;

(B) must specify a reasonable time, place, and manner for the inspection and for performing the related acts; and

(C) may specify the form or forms in which electronically stored information is to be produced.

(2) Responses and Objections.

(A) Time to Respond. The party to whom the request is directed must respond in writing within 30 days after being served. A shorter or longer time may be stipulated to under Rule 29 or be ordered by the court.

(B) Responding to Each Item. For each item or category, the response must either state that inspection and related activities will be permitted as requested or state an objection to the request, including the reasons.

(C) Objections. An objection to part of a request must specify the part and permit inspection of the rest.

(D) Responding to a Request for Production of Electronically Stored Information. The response may state an objection to a requested form for producing electronically stored information. If the responding party objects to a requested form—or if no form was specified in the request—the party must state the form or forms it intends to use.

(E) Producing the Documents or Electronically Stored Information. Unless otherwise stipulated or ordered by the court, these procedures apply to producing documents or electronically stored information:

    (i) A party must produce documents as they are kept in the usual course of business or must organize and label them to correspond to the categories in the request; [and]

    (ii) If a request does not specify a form for producing electronically stored information, a party must produce it in a form or forms in which it is ordinarily maintained or in a reasonably usable form or forms. . . .

(c) Nonparties. As provided in Rule 45, a nonparty may be compelled to produce documents and tangible things or to permit an inspection.

▶ Rule 56. Summary Judgment

(a) A party may move for summary judgment, identifying each claim or defense—or the part of each claim or defense—on which summary judgment is sought. The court shall grant summary judgment if the movant shows that there is no genuine dispute as to any material fact and the movant is entitled to judgment as a matter of law. The court

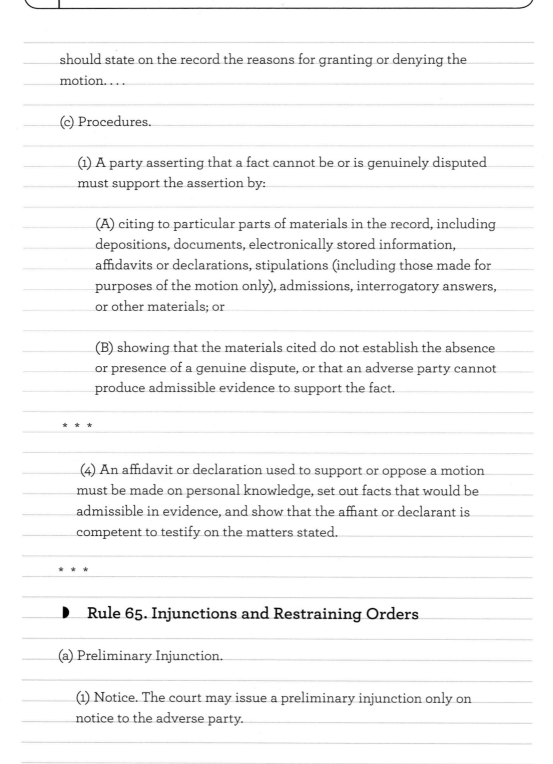

should state on the record the reasons for granting or denying the motion. . . .

(c) Procedures.

(1) A party asserting that a fact cannot be or is genuinely disputed must support the assertion by:

(A) citing to particular parts of materials in the record, including depositions, documents, electronically stored information, affidavits or declarations, stipulations (including those made for purposes of the motion only), admissions, interrogatory answers, or other materials; or

(B) showing that the materials cited do not establish the absence or presence of a genuine dispute, or that an adverse party cannot produce admissible evidence to support the fact.

* * *

(4) An affidavit or declaration used to support or oppose a motion must be made on personal knowledge, set out facts that would be admissible in evidence, and show that the affiant or declarant is competent to testify on the matters stated.

* * *

▶ **Rule 65. Injunctions and Restraining Orders**

(a) Preliminary Injunction.

(1) Notice. The court may issue a preliminary injunction only on notice to the adverse party.

(2) Consolidating the Hearing with the Trial on the Merits. Before or after beginning the hearing on a motion for a preliminary injunction, the court may advance the trial on the merits and consolidate it with the hearing. Even when consolidation is not ordered, evidence that is received on the motion and that would be admissible at trial becomes part of the trial record and need not be repeated at trial. But the court must preserve any party's right to a jury trial.

* * *

(b) Temporary Restraining Order.

(1) Issuing Without Notice. The court may issue a temporary restraining order without written or oral notice to the adverse party or its attorney only if:

(A) specific facts in an affidavit or a verified complaint clearly show that immediate and irreparable injury, loss, or damage will result to the movant before the adverse party can be heard in opposition; and

(B) the movant's attorney certifies in writing any efforts made to give notice and the reasons why it should not be required.

(2) Contents; Expiration. Every temporary restraining order issued without notice must state the date and hour it was issued. . . . The order expires at the time after entry—not to exceed 14 days—that the court sets, unless before that time the court, for good cause, extends it for a like period or the adverse party consents to a longer extension. . . .

(3) Expediting the Preliminary-Injunction Hearing. If the order is issued without notice, the motion for a preliminary injunction must be set for hearing at the earliest possible time. . . .

(4) Motion to Dissolve. On 2 days' notice to the party who obtained the order without notice—or on shorter notice set by the court—the adverse party may appear and move to dissolve or modify the order. The court must then hear and decide the motion as promptly as justice requires.

(c) Security. The court may issue a preliminary injunction or a temporary restraining order only if the movant gives security in an amount that the court considers proper to pay the costs and damages sustained by any party found to have been wrongfully enjoined or restrained. The United States, its officers, and its agencies are not required to give security.

(d) Contents and Scope of Every Injunction and Restraining Order.

(1) Every order granting an injunction and every restraining order must:

(A) state the reasons why it issued;

(B) state its terms specifically; and

(C) describe in reasonable detail—and not by referring to the complaint or other document—the act or acts restrained or required.

(2) The order binds only the following who receive actual notice of it by personal service or otherwise:

(A) the parties;

(B) the parties' officers, agents, servants, employees, and attorneys; and

(C) other persons who are in active concert or participation with anyone described in Rule 65(d)(2)(A) or (B).

* * *

Administrative Procedure Act (and Freedom of Information Act)

▶ **5 U.S.C. § 552—Public information; agency rules, opinions, orders, records, and proceedings (Freedom of Information Act)**

(a) Each agency shall make available to the public information as follows:

* * *

(3) (A) ... [E]ach agency, upon any request for records which

(i) reasonably describes such records and

(ii) is made in accordance with published rules stating the time, place, fees (if any), and procedures to be followed, shall make the records promptly available to any person.

(B) In making any record available to a person under this paragraph, an agency shall provide the record in any form or format requested by the person if the record is readily reproducible by the agency in that form or format. Each agency shall make reasonable efforts to maintain its records in forms or formats that are reproducible for purposes of this section.

(C) In responding under this paragraph to a request for records, an agency shall make reasonable efforts to search for the records in electronic form or format, except when such efforts would significantly interfere with the operation of the agency's automated information system.

(D) For purposes of this paragraph, the term "search" means to review, manually or by automated means, agency records for the purpose of locating those records which are responsive to a request....

(4) (A) (i) In order to carry out the provisions of this section, each agency shall promulgate regulations, pursuant to notice and receipt of public comment, specifying the schedule of fees applicable to the processing of requests under this section and establishing procedures and guidelines for determining when such fees should be waived or reduced....

(iii) Documents shall be furnished without any charge or at a [reduced] charge... if disclosure of the information is in the public interest because it is likely to contribute significantly to public understanding of the operations or activities of the government and is not primarily in the commercial interest of the requester.

* * *

(B) On complaint, the district court of the United States in the district in which the complainant resides, or has his principal place of business, or in which the agency records are situated, or in the District of Columbia, has jurisdiction to enjoin the agency from withholding agency records and to order the production of any agency records improperly withheld from the complainant. In such a case the court shall determine the matter de novo, and may examine the contents of such agency records in camera to determine whether such records or any part thereof shall be withheld under any of the exemptions set forth in subsection (b) of this section, and the burden is on the agency to sustain its action. . . .

(i) The court may assess against the United States reasonable attorney fees and other litigation costs reasonably incurred in any case under this section in which the complainant has substantially prevailed.

(ii) For purposes of this subparagraph, a complainant has substantially prevailed if the complainant has obtained relief through either—

(I) a judicial order, or an enforceable written agreement or consent decree; or

(II) a voluntary or unilateral change in position by the agency, if the complainant's claim is not insubstantial.

* * *

(6) (A) Each agency, upon any request for records made under paragraph (1), (2), or (3) of this subsection, shall—

(i) determine within 20 days (excepting Saturdays, Sundays, and legal public holidays) after the receipt of any such request whether to comply with such request and shall immediately notify the person making such request of such determination and the reasons therefor, and of the right of such person to appeal to the head of the agency any adverse determination. . . .

* * *

(b) This section does not apply to matters that are—

(1) (A) specifically authorized under criteria established by an Executive order to be kept secret in the interest of national defense or foreign policy and (B) are in fact properly classified pursuant to such Executive order;

(2) related solely to the internal personnel rules and practices of an agency;

(3) specifically exempted from disclosure by statute . . . .

(4) trade secrets and commercial or financial information obtained from a person and privileged or confidential;

(5) inter-agency or intra-agency memorandums or letters which would not be available by law to a party other than an agency in litigation with the agency;

(6) personnel and medical files and similar files the disclosure of which would constitute a clearly unwarranted invasion of personal privacy;

(7) records or information compiled for law enforcement purposes . . . .

(9) geological and geophysical information and data, including maps, concerning wells.

* * *

(f) For purposes of this section, the term—

(1) "agency" as defined in section 551 (1) of this title includes any executive department, military department, Government corporation, Government controlled corporation, or other establishment in the executive branch of the Government (including the Executive Office of the President), or any independent regulatory agency; and

(2) "record" and any other term used in this section in reference to information includes—

(A) any information that would be an agency record subject to the requirements of this section when maintained by an agency in any format, including an electronic format; and

(B) any information described under subparagraph (A) that is maintained for an agency by an entity under Government contract, for the purposes of records management.

* * *

▶ 5 U.S.C. § 553. Rule making

(a) This section applies, according to the provisions thereof, except to the extent that there is involved -

(1) a military or foreign affairs function of the United States; or

(2) a matter relating to agency management or personnel or to public property, loans, grants, benefits, or contracts.

(b) General notice of proposed rule making shall be published in the Federal Register, unless persons subject thereto are named and either personally served or otherwise have actual notice thereof in accordance with law. The notice shall include—

>   (1) a statement of the time, place, and nature of public rule making proceedings;

>   (2) reference to the legal authority under which the rule is proposed; and

>   (3) either the terms or substance of the proposed rule or a description of the subjects and issues involved.

Except when notice or hearing is required by statute, this subsection does not apply—

>   (A) to interpretative rules, general statements of policy, or rules of agency organization, procedure, or practice; or

>   (B) when the agency for good cause finds (and incorporates the finding and a brief statement of reasons therefore in the rules issued) that notice and public procedure thereon are impracticable, unnecessary, or contrary to the public interest.

(c) After notice required by this section, the agency shall give interested persons an opportunity to participate in the rule making through submission of written data, views, or arguments with or without opportunity for oral presentation. After consideration of the relevant matter presented, the agency shall incorporate in the rules adopted a concise general statement of their basis and purpose….

  * * *

(e) Each agency shall give an interested person the right to petition for the issuance, amendment, or repeal of a rule.

▶   **5 U.S.C. § 702. Right of review**

A person suffering legal wrong because of agency action, or adversely affected or aggrieved by agency action within the meaning of a relevant statute, is entitled to judicial review thereof.

▶   **5 U.S.C. § 704. Actions reviewable**

Agency action made reviewable by statute and final agency action for which there is no other adequate remedy in a court are subject to judicial review. . . .

▶   **5 U.S.C. § 706. Scope of review**

To the extent necessary to decision and when presented, the reviewing court shall decide all relevant questions of law, interpret constitutional and statutory provisions, and determine the meaning or applicability of the terms of an agency action. The reviewing court shall—

(1) compel agency action unlawfully withheld or unreasonably delayed; and

(2) hold unlawful and set aside agency action, findings, and conclusions found to be—

(A) arbitrary, capricious, an abuse of discretion, or otherwise not in accordance with law;

(B) contrary to constitutional right, power, privilege, or immunity;

(C) in excess of statutory jurisdiction, authority, or limitations, or short of statutory right;

(D) without observance of procedure required by law;

(E) unsupported by substantial evidence in a case subject to sections 556 and 557 of this title or otherwise reviewed on the record of an agency hearing provided by statute; or

(F) unwarranted by the facts to the extent that the facts are subject to trial de novo by the reviewing court.

In making the foregoing determinations, the court shall review the whole record or those parts of it cited by a party, and due account shall be taken of the rule of prejudicial error.

Appendix C
Form: Time Sheets

Attorney:

Client:

Billing No.

DATE	DESCRIPTION	TIME

Form: Time Sheets

Attorney:

Client:

Billing No.

DATE	DESCRIPTION	TIME

Form: Time Sheets

Attorney:

Client:

Billing No.

DATE	DESCRIPTION	TIME

Form: Time Sheets

Attorney:
Client:
Billing No.

DATE	DESCRIPTION	TIME

Form: Time Sheets

Attorney:

Client:

Billing No.

DATE	DESCRIPTION	TIME

Form: Time Sheets

Attorney:
Client:
Billing No.

DATE	DESCRIPTION	TIME